COSMIC CONVERGENCE

JOURNEYS OF WALK-INS, STARSEEDS AND HYBRIDS

COSMIC CONVERGENCE

JOURNEYS OF WALK-INS, STARSEEDS AND HYBRIDS

SHEILA SEPPI AND **BARBARA LAMB**

FOREWORD BY MARY RODWELL

Books may be purchased through booksellers or by contacting Sacred Stories Publishing.

Cosmic Convergence
Journeys of Walk-Ins, Starseeds, and Hybrids

Sheila Seppi and Barbara Lamb

Tradepaper ISBN: 978-1-958921-70-8
Electronic Book ISBN 978-1-958921-71-5

Library of Congress Control Number: 2024946257

Published by Haniel Press

An Imprint of Sacred Stories Publishing, Fort Lauderdale, FL

Printed in the United States of America

DEDICATION

This book is dedicated to all the walk-ins, starseeds, and hybrids that have come to Earth to help anchor new energies for the paradigm shift.

Thank you, brave souls, for being here.

TABLE OF CONTENTS

Foreword 1

The Emergence of Walk-Ins, Starseeds, and Hybrids 5
The Infinite Realms 13
Universal Multidimensionality 31
The Holographic Fields 47

SECTION ONE: WALK-INS
Dance of the Soul 71
Hypnotic Regression Therapy 97
Walk-In Hypnotic Regression Session #1 101
Walk-In Hypnotic Regression Session #2 105
Walk-In Hypnotic Regression Session #3 109
Walk-In Hypnotic Regression Session #4 113
Walk-In Hypnotic Regression Session #5 117
A New Reality 121

SECTION TWO: STARSEEDS
Exploring the Cosmic Origins of Human Souls 127
Starseed Hypnotic Regression: Session #1 139
Starseed Hypnotic Regression Session #2 143
Starseed Hypnotic Regression Session #3 147
Starseed Hypnotic Regression Session #4 151
Starseed Hypnotic Regression Session #5 155
Starseed Hypnotic Regression Session #6 159
Echoes of the Stars 161

SECTION THREE: HYBRIDS

The Dawn of the New Human 167

Awakening the Hybrid Secret 183

Hybrid Hypnotic Regression Session #1 189

Hybrid Hypnotic Regression Session #2 193

Hybrid Hypnotic Regression Session #3 197

Hybrid Hypnotic Regression Session #4 201

Hybrid Hypnotic Regression Session #5 205

Crossroads of Creation 209

Embracing the Cosmic Tapestry 211

Glossary of Terms..215

Meet the Authors...223

FOREWORD

It is my pleasure and honor to write the foreword to *Cosmic Convergence: The Journeys of Walk-ins, Starseeds, and Hybrids,* authored by Sheila Seppi and Barbara Lamb. In my opinion this comprehensive and enlightening book has the depth of information to help not only the more awake souls who will find a resonance within its pages but especially help the newly awakened who seek deeper understanding and answers to their unfolding human journey and connect the dots as to why they always felt so different to their family and society in general. Many are struggling to fit into a society that, in many cases, can feel quite alien. They often have a deep longing to go home but not always knowing where home might be and unable to understand why they feel this so deeply in their soul. In many cases they are consciously and multidimensionally aware of communication and contact with numerous intelligences and life forms that reside in the multiverses and in other realms of existence. *Cosmic Convergence* is a book that can help to explain many of these feelings with information to answer such questions as it explores in depth the matrix of the soul.

I have deep respect for both authors of *Cosmic Convergence* as friends and colleagues on a similar path to my own. Barbara Lamb is author of *Crop Circles Revealed, Alien Experiences,* and *Meet the Hybrids* and Sheila

Seppi is the author of *Walk-Ins Cosmology of the Soul*. Both authors have gleaned a wealth of knowledge, both experientially and through their work with individuals, as these previous books suggest. In *Cosmic Convergence*, Barbara Lamb and Sheila Seppi have expanded their research exploring in greater depth the understanding gleaned not only from personal exploration in the case of Sheila Seppi, but detailed and corroborative information gained through regression hypnosis. Barbara Lamb alone has regressed several thousand individuals in her long career in this field. The results from both sources and regressions reveal concepts of realities the soul can exist in and demonstrate the incredibly complex nature of what we term the soul. Information that suggests that within the multiverse what we understand as multidimensional, interdimensional, and extradimensional journeys and existences beyond space time are concepts explained and understood through our higher consciousness or oversoul. However, many of us are only beginning to have some deeper understanding of this complexity as we personally explore our inner reality and tap into our superconscious, higher self-awareness, and intuitive abilities through personal development such as meditation, shamanic journeys, out of body experiences (OBE), near-death experience (NDE), remote viewing (RV), healing modalities, or regression hypnosis.

In my personal research as Principal of the Australian Close Encounter Resource Network, I work as a counselor and hypnotherapist and have gathered information from individuals, both in conscious recall and hypnosis, which has elicited often identical information as is explored in *Cosmic Convergence*, although not with such clarity and depth. As a hypnotherapist accessing the subconscious / superconscious, I found that extraordinary information can be elicited that not only taps into the present life but into what we term past lives (although we are also told time doesn't exist as such and all is occurring now). However, what can be revealed in many instances is termed past lives and indicates that the soul essence always survives, even when the physical body dies. This concept has been explored in detail by many researchers including me, exploring the soul journey in "life between lives." However, *Cosmic Convergence* takes this understanding to another level and exposes the many realms and special nature of a particular soul and its specific origins. It may well answer multiple feelings and knowings that the reader has experienced or felt deeply about themselves and so validate and connect the dots in their own personal journey.

Cosmic Convergence brings in many concepts under three headings—walk-ins, starseeds, and hybrids—that are more familiar to many awake and awakening souls. But what may be new to some readers are explanations and understanding of the terms such as Earth Seeds, Fey Souls, Dragon Souls, Angelic Souls, Dimensional Starseeds, Interdimensional Souls, Wanderer Souls, and Star children whose lineage show through their auras indicating they are either Indigo Children, Rainbow Children, Crystal Children, etc.

In their research, the authors have encapsulated specific terms highlighting the depth and complexity of the different roles and mandates the souls may have in this incarnation at this time on Gaia, heralding the awakening of humanity in which they have chosen to participate and their specific role and soul mission on Gaia at this time.

For anyone who reads *Cosmic Convergence*, such as individuals who can relate to the terms and understanding, it will offer reassurance. For those still exploring and awakening, the information may well be significant as they explore. It offers an opportunity for more resonance and confirmation in their personal journey. The accounts shared explain how we each operate and experience our lives through a soul consciousness and how it manifests in each individual soul as well as the source of this awareness and how our soul origin guides the path to spiritual growth and spiritual expansion on the journey back to Source.

What makes *Cosmic Convergence* unique, from my perspective as a researcher and seeker, is the depth in which both authors have studied the phenomenon as well as the honesty and courage of sharing personal experiences. Barbara Lamb has been recognized as a leading researcher and therapist in the field of Ufology for many, many years and is highly respected globally. Her work in regression hypnosis with Experiencers (individuals who have experienced Contact with Non-Human Intelligences or NHIs) has offered significant insight into the Contact Phenomenon that has been crucial in helping the public understand the complexity of humanity's interactions with NHIs. Sheila Seppi, with her own personal journey as a soul-exchange walk-in, entered the body of a thirty-eight-year-old mother with three children and healed her from life-threatening disease instantaneously. This book represents a wonderful combination of shared wisdom and knowledge from these two special souls.

I have a deep respect for both authors and celebrate this latest research as it adds even more depth to what we have communicated and shared over the years. I applaud their dedication and commitment coupled with their deep understanding and knowledge of the subjects explored in *Cosmic Convergence*. This is a book that shines an extraordinary light into the soul as it offers a greater understanding of who and what we really are. Enjoy this expansive, enlightening, and exciting journey through sharing and the light of *Cosmic Convergence*.

Mary Rodwell, Founder and Principal of Australian Close Encounter Resource Network (ACERN)
Co-Founder of Dr. Edgar Mitchell (FREE) Foundation
Author of *Awakening: How Extraterrestrial Contact Can Transform Your Life (2002)* and *The New Human: Awakening to Our Cosmic Heritage (2016)*

THE EMERGENCE OF WALK-INS, STARSEEDS, AND HYBRIDS

In the kaleidoscope of human experience, where the boundaries of reality blur and the mysteries of the cosmos beckon, there exists a phenomenon that challenges the very fabric of our understanding—the emergence of walk-ins, starseeds, and hybrids. These alchemical beings traverse the realms of human consciousness, embodying a synthesis of terrestrial and extraterrestrial origins and carrying within them the seeds of transformation and evolution.

At the heart of the phenomenon of *walk-ins* lies the soul exchange—an extraordinary occurrence in which one soul vacates a human vessel, allowing another soul to inhabit it. This concept, rooted in ancient spiritual traditions, suggests that souls may enter and exit physical bodies guided by a higher purpose or a Divine plan. One cannot request that a walk-in event occurs in their life, as these events are preordained. They happen for a purpose, including to help anchor higher frequencies on the planet.

For those who experience a walk-in event, the process is often described as a profound awakening—a sudden and unexpected shift in consciousness that alters the trajectory of their lives forever. In some cases, the individual may have no memory of their previous identity, while in others, they retain fragments of their former self that serve as a bridge between past and present. Others retain full memories and the personality of the form they inhabit.

The origins of walk-ins are shrouded in mystery, with theories ranging from interdimensional origins to cosmically bound agreements made before they were born. Some believe that walk-ins are souls from other realms, dimensions, universes, or planets who have volunteered to incarnate on Earth to assist in humanity's spiritual evolution. Others suggest that walk-ins may be beings of light or higher consciousness who have chosen to enter human bodies to fulfill a specific mission or purpose. Regardless, each walk-in event is different and unique to the individual, and each walk-in is from a much higher vibrational dimension or density than the previous soul.

Closely related to the concept of walk-ins are *starseeds*—individuals believed to be souls originating from distant celestial realms or planets who have chosen to incarnate on Earth to assist in its spiritual evolution. Like seeds scattered upon fertile soil, starseeds bring with them the wisdom and energy of their cosmic origins. They serve as beacons of light in a world shrouded in darkness, and their spiritual ideas sprout to enlighten humanity.

Starseeds also often feel a deep sense of longing or homesickness for their true cosmic home as well as a compelling sense of purpose or mission on Earth. They may possess psychic abilities or heightened intuition and may be drawn to spiritual practices or metaphysical teachings that resonate with their soul's journey.

The concept of starseeds has gained popularity in recent years, fueled by the growing interest in spirituality and the search for meaning in an increasingly complex world. Many believe that starseeds are here to help humanity awaken to its true potential by guiding us toward a higher level of consciousness and collective understanding.

Hybrids occupy a unique and intriguing position: They are beings whose genetic makeup incorporates elements from both human and non-human sources. Whether the result of genetic engineering, extraterrestrial intervention, or a natural evolutionary process, hybrids challenge our understanding of what it means to be human, blurring the lines between species and worlds.

Hybrids may possess a wide range of physical and psychic abilities as well as a heightened sensitivity to subtle energies and vibrations. They may feel a sense of displacement or alienation in the world as well as a deep longing to connect with others who share their unique heritage.

For some, the emergence of hybrids represents a new chapter in human evolution—a potential glimpse into our collective future as a species. By embracing our hybrid nature and transcending the limitations of conventional identity, we may unlock the hidden potentials within ourselves and usher in a new era of harmony and understanding.

As we navigate the territories of walk-ins, starseeds, and hybrids, we are confronted with questions about the nature of reality, consciousness, and our place in the cosmos. What does it mean to be human in a universe teeming with life and intelligence? How do we reconcile the limitations of our physical existence with the boundless potential of our spiritual nature? These are the questions of our time.

In the end, perhaps the answers lie not in the realm of the intellect but in the depths of the heart—in the timeless wisdom that whispers to us from beyond the veil of ordinary perception. In the exploration of these phenomena, we may discover not only the secrets of our past but also the keys to unlocking our future.

As we stand upon the threshold of a new era of human consciousness, let us embrace the diversity and complexity of the human experience, celebrating the tapestry of life that braids us all together. For in the presence of walk-ins, starseeds, and hybrids, we may find the seeds of our own awakening—the promise of a brighter tomorrow, rooted in the infinite potential of the human spirit.

In the chapters that follow, you will find a rich weaving of information and insights into the fascinating realms of walk-ins, starseeds, and hybrids. These phenomena offer us a glimpse into the vast and mysterious landscape of human consciousness and the cosmos beyond. The main content was written by Sheila Seppi; Barbara Lamb wrote the accounts of hypnotic regressions.

This book opens by delving into the intricate and interconnected concepts of dimensions, densities, and the harmonic universe, forming the foundation for our exploration of cosmic convergence. The explanations of these concepts aim to unravel the complexity and mystery of the universe, highlighting the intricate connections that shape our reality.

Density signifies the varying states of matter and energy, while *dimensions* denote distinct levels of perception and consciousness, allowing for movement between different planes of existence. The *harmonic universe* introduces a layered structure of interconnected realities, each with its own vibrational frequency and state of consciousness. Understanding these principles is essential for navigating the paths of our cosmic journey and grasping the deeper aspects of our universal fabric. This knowledge will prove essential in understanding the information that follows.

Universal multidimensionality describes the vast and multifaceted realms of existence by delving deeply into the seven planes of existence, offering insights into the distinct levels of reality and consciousness that shape our universe. Additionally, *multidimensionality* explores the fascinating concepts of parallel universes and timelines, unveiling the intricate web of alternate realities and potential paths that coexist alongside our own. By understanding these ideas, readers will gain a greater appreciation for the interconnectedness of all things and the endless possibilities that lie within the fabric of the cosmos. These concepts will help explain how the journeys of walk-ins, starseeds, and hybrids are possible.

Matrix fields are diverse vibrational manifestations within the human holographic field, including the intricate dynamics of the spiritual bodies, the aura, chakras, ley lines, meridians—especially as they apply to the profound transformations that accompany walk-in experiences, starseed awakenings, and hybrid realizations. This chapter offers a detailed exploration of how each component—spiritual bodies, aura, and the holographic field—is a distinct element that also functions in synergy, adapting to the unique vibrational shifts that these extraordinary events trigger.

Following these explanations, you will find three distinct sections; each section begins with an overview providing readers with essential context and understanding. Here we delve into walk-in, starseed, and hybrid experiences uncovered through hypnotic regression accounts conducted by Barbara Lamb. The regressions offer an intimate glimpse into the lives and journeys of those who have had these transformational experiences. Finally, we draw upon these narratives to suggest a conclusion that reflects the deeper implications of these encounters for humanity's understanding of identity, consciousness, and the universe itself.

SECTION ONE: WALK-INS

Our journey begins with an examination of walk-ins, individuals who undergo a soul exchange or other type of soul experience where their natal soul (original soul) is augmented or exchanged. Through compelling narratives and firsthand accounts detailed through hypnotic regression sessions, we illuminate the transformative nature of these experiences, shedding light on the important shifts in consciousness and identity that accompany them.

We will delve into the complexities of walk-ins' existence from the moment of arrival to the integration process that follows, exploring their unique perspectives and contributions to the collective human experience. We also will look at the soul's progression from its division from the original Source self to incarnation. This is an expanded version of Anatomy of the Spirit from my first book, *Walk-Ins: Cosmology of the Soul*. There we discuss several types of walk-in soul experiences followed by soul origins. Next, individuals provide, under hypnosis, their accounts of becoming a walk-in.

SECTION TWO: STARSEEDS

Next, we turn our gaze to starseeds, cosmic beings who incarnate on Earth with a mission and purpose derived from their celestial origins. We will discuss the origins and through hypnotic regression sessions and personal testimonials, we uncover the cosmic connections and earthly missions that define the starseed experience. From their inherent wisdom to their innate sense of purpose, we delve into the multifaceted nature of starseeds, offering insights into their role in guiding humanity toward a higher state of consciousness and evolution.

SECTION THREE: HYBRIDS

In the final leg of our journey, we will explore the phenomenon of hybrids— beings embodying both human and extraterrestrial traits. Through hypnotic exploration and firsthand accounts, we navigate the complexities of hybrid existence, unraveling the intricacies of their cosmic lineage and earthly manifestations. From their unique physical attributes to their intense need for a sense of belonging, we delve into the hybrid experience, offering glimpses into their role in bridging the gap between humanity and the cosmos.

With the narratives and insights gleaned from our exploration, we can weave together a comprehensive conclusion that reflects on the profound implications of these encounters for our understanding of identity, consciousness, and the universe itself. Through the lens of walk-ins, starseeds, and hybrids, we contemplate the interconnectedness of all things and the transformative power of cosmic encounters in shaping the human experience.

At the conclusion of our discussion, readers will find a comprehensive glossary of terms, which the reader might want to review before beginning the first chapter or refer to whenever they encounter an unknown term. It provides definitions and explanations for key concepts that are discussed throughout the book.

As a side note to you, the reader, I would like to share my personal story.

I entered the physical body of Sheila in 1999 through a soul-exchange walk-in experience. Since then, I've maintained a connection with what I call "my collective." The collective comprises many multidimensional facets of my oversoul, reassembled from numerous individual soul experiences into a single unified consciousness. This consciousness, spanning realms, star systems and universes, encompasses individuated soul aspects from the angelic realm and the Pleiadian, Lyran, Sirian, Arcturian, Mantis, Vega, Orion, and Andromedan star systems, to name a few. Together, these unified soul fragments form what I fondly refer to as my collective. Our collective name is Yahni. Many members of the collective have worked through me, Sheila, during the writing of this book to bring their words onto these pages. One member, an Andromedan Elder Mother, Tiamu, has channeled light language into its pages. She is a future aspect of my Andromedan self.

Prior to my embodiment, the collective was called from the Andromedan system to assist Gaia, Mother Earth, with the repair of the etheric crystalline grid that surrounds the planet. We merged our consciousness with the consciousness of those already working on the grid to repair and send an infusion of light codes of awakening, unconditional love, and unity consciousness. When the natal or original soul of the Sheila body cried out that it was time to be released, it was decided by the collective that I would be the individuated soul aspect to enter that body.

Throughout this book, I will frequently refer to my expanded consciousness as my collective, as they play a significant role in shaping my experiences and understanding of the universe and life on Earth.

It is our hope that the insights gained from these chapters serve as a catalyst for further exploration and discovery, inspiring you to delve deeper into the mysteries that lie at the heart of our existence. For in the pursuit of knowledge and understanding, we may uncover not only the secrets of the universe but also the key to unlocking our true individual potential as beings of light and love.

So let us begin the journey with open hearts and curious minds, guided by the light of truth and the wisdom of the ages. For in the exploration of hypnosis, walk-ins, starseeds, and hybrids, we may find the answers we seek and the transformation we so earnestly desire.

Your adventure awaits.

THE INFINITE REALMS

In the vast tapestry of the cosmos, the concepts of dimensions, densities, and harmonic universes weave a narrative both complex and mysterious. These ideas reflect the interconnectedness as well as the nature and purpose that compel walk-ins, starseeds, and hybrids. These foundational ideas are crucial for understanding the intricate paths we travel in the journey of our soul's evolution through cosmic convergence.

The concepts of dimensions and densities are often used interchangeably in metaphysical and spiritual discussions, but they have distinct meanings, particularly when discussing consciousness and the structure of reality. Understanding these distinctions can clarify how these concepts relate to each other and to the evolution of consciousness.

Please note that the following descriptions are my interpretations from information provided and verified to me by my collective and the higher-consciousness beings that I work with. They are not meant to be comprehensive but to provide a framework from which one can begin to understand the differences between these concepts.

Dimensions refer to different perceptions of reality, each with its own unique properties and rules. They are often thought of as layers of existence. Dimensions are not physical spaces but states of reality. Each layer describes both a perception and how we operate within that reality.

Densities are spaces that vibrate at different frequency rates and help describe the evolution of consciousness. They are like a cup that holds the waters of each dimension.

Harmonic universes describe the organization of dimensions and densities into structured layers of reality, each with its own unique vibrational frequency, integrating the element of time, the evolution of consciousness, and the type of beings that operate within each.

As we explore the realms of walk-ins, starseeds, and hybrids, it is essential to delve deep into these concepts, as they set the stage for the transformative experiences and revelations that follow.

DIMENSIONS: PERCEPTIONS OF REALITY

Dimensions extend far beyond the conventional understanding of space and time. They offer insights into the multifaceted nature of reality and consciousness.

Humanity operates within twelve dimensions. Dimensions inherently link us to distinct facets of existence and understandings, offering opportunities to perceive, engage with, and integrate them into our current reality. Each dimension contains twelve sub-dimensions, layers or octaves of reality within it, ranging from the lowest to the highest octave of understanding and mastery. As we fully understand and integrate each dimension, we advance to a deeper perception of understanding, progressively evolving until we can grasp all twelve simultaneously.

Below is a broad overview of the twelve primary dimensions, each more complex and spiritually evolved than the one preceding it.

Dimension One: The first dimension is the most basic and foundational level of existence, characterized by the presence of length, but no other spatial properties. It holds the introduction of a straight line.

Consciousness here is quite rudimentary and is all about the physical.

Dimension Two: The second dimension adds an additional spatial property, height, creating a two-dimensional plane. In this dimension, you begin to see shapes, such as a square.

Consciousness here is basic and focuses on biological consciousness with no identity of self and is associated with more basic or elemental forms of life and existence, such as plants and lower animals.

Dimension Three: This is the dimension where matter takes shape, marking the realm of physicality populated by humans. In this dimension, humans often perceive themselves as separate entities, disconnected from their true essence. The third dimension encompasses the physical reality experienced through the five senses and serves as a school for learning and spiritual evolution. This dimension offers opportunities for growth through various challenges and experiences.

Third-dimensional human consciousness, often referred to as 3D consciousness, is characterized by a perception of reality that is based on physical and material aspects. This state of consciousness is predominantly focused on the tangible and sensory experiences of the world. In 3D consciousness, individuals typically perceive their identity and reality within a framework of separation and duality—seeing themselves as distinct from others and from the environment.

This level of consciousness is governed by linear time (past, present, future) and is heavily influenced by societal norms, cultural conditioning, and ego-driven pursuits. People operating primarily in 3D consciousness may prioritize material success, personal power, and the fulfillment of desires that serve the individual self rather than the collective good.

Furthermore, 3D consciousness involves reactive emotional states where feelings such as fear, jealousy, and anger are more common. These emotions are frequently driven by the ego's perception of threat or loss related to the physical or social environment.

The journey of spiritual and personal development involves expanding beyond 3D consciousness to higher dimensions of awareness, where the interconnectedness of all life and the non-physical aspects of existence become more apparent and influential. Additionally, the elemental realm can be found here.

Dimension Four: This is the dimension of time, where matter becomes etheric once more, but time remains linear. Often referred to as the *astral plane*, the fourth dimension is the realm of the subconscious mind, where psychic abilities manifest and the soul resides. It transcends physical limitations associated with non-physical phenomena such as dreams, emotions, and psychic experiences. This dimension introduces a greater understanding of love, compassion, and community, emphasizing personal transformation and the initial stages of spiritual awakening.

Fourth-dimension (4D) human consciousness is about transpersonal awareness and represents an evolution beyond the typical physical and material preoccupations of the third dimension. It is often associated with the astral plane and emotional release.

In 4D consciousness, time is experienced more fluidly, with an increased awareness of the past, present, and future as interconnected rather than strictly linear. This dimension introduces a deeper understanding of the intangible aspects of existence, such as thoughts, emotions, and energies, which are recognized as influential forces that shape one's reality.

Individuals operating within 4D consciousness begin to see themselves and others as part of a larger, interconnected whole, reducing feelings of separation. This awareness often leads to deeper empathy and compassion, as well as a desire to live in harmony with others and the environment. Additionally, manifestations and synchronicities become more apparent, as people in 4D are more attuned to how their thoughts and intentions can directly influence their physical surroundings and experiences.

Furthermore, 4D consciousness is marked by a transitional phase toward spiritual awakening, where individuals may start to question traditional societal structures and their own life purpose. This dimension serves as a bridge to even higher states of consciousness, where the unity of all existence is fully realized and embraced.

In addition to humans, this dimension is inhabited by astral beings, spirits, and entities beyond the physical realm, including guides, guardians, and departed souls navigating the astral plane. Planes of existence and the beings that inhabit them are discussed in more detail in the next chapter.

Dimension Five: Representing unified consciousness through higher consciousness and expanded awareness, the fifth dimension is often described as a state of interconnectedness transcending duality and separation. Time is fluid here.

This level marks a significant transcendence from the ego, focusing on unity and oneness. Beings in 5D operate from a state of unconditional love, experiencing less physicality and greater light, and possessing the ability to manifest and heal more intuitively.

Fifth-dimension (5D) human consciousness marks a transformation in the way individuals perceive and interact with the world. It is characterized by a deep sense of unity and oneness with all that exists. In 5D consciousness, the perception of separation between oneself and others—including nature and the universe—dissolves, fostering a deep, intrinsic understanding of interconnectedness and interdependence.

In this state, individuals operate from a place of unconditional love, compassion, and empathy, not just for other humans but for all forms of life. The ego-driven desires and fears that dominate lower levels of consciousness are significantly diminished, leading to a life guided by higher spiritual and universal principles.

Fifth-dimensional consciousness also transcends traditional notions of time and space, allowing for a more significant experience of the present moment as timeless and infinite. This shift enables profound peace and contentment, as individuals are no longer bound by the constraints of past regrets or future anxieties.

Additionally, those experiencing 5D consciousness often report enhanced intuition, psychic abilities, and a direct connection to Divine energies. Manifestation becomes more effortless, governed by the alignment with the soul's purpose and the greater good rather than personal gain.

This expansive state of consciousness reflects not only a personal transformation but also suggests the potential for a collective shift toward a more harmonious and enlightened existence.

Dimension Six: Archetypal patterns, cosmic laws, and Divine intelligence are located here. The sixth dimension holds the consciousness of the light body. This dimension is associated with higher mental faculties, intuition, and spiritual guidance. It involves a mastery of spiritual wisdom and the ability to navigate different dimensions.

As for human consciousness, the sixth dimension represents a level of spiritual evolution and understanding beyond personal and planetary scope. In 6D, consciousness is primarily focused on unity, cosmic awareness, and the integration of spiritual and physical realities.

Individuals operating at this level are deeply committed to the principles of universal love and unconditional service. They are motivated by a selfless desire to assist in the spiritual evolution of all beings, transcending personal or even planetary concerns. There is an acute awareness of the interconnectedness of all life forms across different dimensions and galaxies. Beings in 6D consciousness perceive and interact with the energy and consciousness of a range of entities, from physical beings to more ethereal forms.

Those in 6D consciousness have mastered the art of manifestation, able to create and manipulate realities with precision and for the higher good. Their creations are typically aligned with the universal laws and the principles of spiritual harmony. Time and space are experienced as fluid and malleable; past, present, and future are accessible as a single continuum. This allows for an experience of existence that transcends the linear progression of time as experienced in lower dimensions.

Knowledge in 6D is not accumulated through learning or study but is directly perceived through a connection with the cosmic intelligence. Wisdom is often shared telepathically or through energetic transmissions between beings.

Sixth-dimensional beings are adept at working with complex energy structures of the universe. They can facilitate healing, balance, and ascension processes, not only on an individual level but also on a cosmic scale. It represents a level where the distinctions between individuality and collective existence blur, leading to a harmonious and profound interaction with all aspects of the universe.

Entities in 6D are often seen as guides or teachers for lower dimensions, helping in the cosmic evolution of various beings. It is populated by archetypal energies, cosmic intelligences, and Divine principles, including higher-dimensional beings guiding evolution and spiritual development.

Dimension Seven: This dimension of spiritual realization and enlightenment represents the merging of individual consciousness into cosmic consciousness. It is here that time becomes nonlinear and a connection to the cosmos and its multidimensional aspects begins to emerge.

For most humans, 7D consciousness remains an aspirational concept. It represents a state of being that we may strive toward as part of our spiritual journey but is beyond the current scope of everyday human experience; however, it is not impossible to achieve. It requires a highly advanced state of spiritual evolution and embodies a level of existence where beings have transcended the typical limitations of physical reality, embracing broader cosmic roles and capabilities.

In many spiritual traditions, reaching 7D consciousness is synonymous with achieving ultimate enlightenment or spiritual liberation. This dimension symbolizes the culmination of a soul's journey through the cycles of birth, death, and rebirth. Even though direct experience of 7D consciousness might not be common, its principles influence spiritual teachings and practices. Insights believed to be channeled from beings of this level contribute to humanity's understanding of spiritual principles and help cultivate the broader spiritual evolution of the planet.

In essence, 7D human consciousness is about reaching a level of spiritual existence that is integrated with the highest realities of the universe. It involves transcending all lower forms of existence to engage directly with the cosmic fabric, serving as part of the Divine mechanism that guides and supports all of creation.

Beings who have achieved this state are involved with the harmonic structure of the universe, working with energies that sustain and create planes of existence. The seventh dimension is inhabited by enlightened beings, ascended masters, and embodiments of universal consciousness representing unity and oneness with the Divine.

Dimension Eight: Beyond human comprehension, the eighth dimension (8D) is often described as the realm of Divine consciousness and cosmic unity. It is associated with the realization of one's true nature as a Divine being and is populated by cosmic deities, celestial beings, and Divine manifestations. It is a timeless realm centered on archetypal consciousness, which is dedicated to mastering and comprehending archetypal energies and universal patterns. Beings at this level are often considered the architects of reality, structuring the essence of existence across dimensions.

Dimension Nine: Ninth-dimension (9D) consciousness in human understanding is often described as a level of existence that transcends even the already highly advanced states of spiritual awareness found in lower dimensions. It encompasses realms of cosmic wisdom and a deep, inherent connection to the universal fabric.

The ninth dimension is associated with the highest orders of angels and celestial beings, whose focus is on the service to the Divine plan. These beings enact the will of the cosmos. It represents the integration of all aspects of existence into a unified whole and is inhabited by beings of cosmic harmony, Divine order, and universal balance, including cosmic architects and overseers of universal laws.

Dimension Ten: Tenth-dimension (10D) consciousness represents an extraordinarily advanced stage of spiritual evolution that is characterized by a complete transcendence of all physical and metaphysical limitations previously understood. It is a realm of infinite possibilities and potentiality. The tenth dimension is associated with the manifestation of intentions and the co-creation of reality.

Beings in this dimension are thought to be the architects of cosmic laws, setting the parameters by which entire realities operate. They have infinite potentiality as creator gods and cosmic architects shaping reality, guiding the manifestation of intentions and the co-creation of universes. This includes defining the laws of physics for various dimensions, as well as deeper metaphysical laws.

Tenth-dimension consciousness represents a realm of perfect unity and intense creative power, where beings are no longer distinct entities but integral aspects of a continuous, dynamic expression of the Divine. The tenth dimension is the epitome of spiritual evolution, where the boundaries of individuality and separateness dissolve entirely in the face of absolute oneness with the universe.

Dimension Eleven: Beyond linear time and space, the eleventh dimension (11D) represents the totality of all possible timelines and realities. It is associated with the concept of parallel universes and multidimensional existence (discussed in more detail in the next chapter). The eleventh dimension is inhabited by beings existing beyond linear time and space, who oversee the multiverse and parallel realities and function as universal gateways, managing and synthesizing the interflow of cosmic energies and consciousness across all existing dimensions. They ensure that the multiverse remains coherent and that its diverse realities are aligned with the overarching Divine blueprint.

The beings operating within this dimension have an omnipresent awareness, being simultaneously aware of all happenings across multiple dimensions and realities. This supreme level of awareness allows them to orchestrate complex cosmic events and processes, and to manipulate these constructs in ways that are unfathomable to lower-dimensional consciousness, such as reversing time or instantaneously altering vast expanses of space.

The consciousness here is one of ultimate peacemaking and the beings sometimes serve to resolve conflicts and discrepancies that arise within the multiverse, ensuring that the evolution of consciousness proceeds smoothly across various levels of existence.

Dimension Twelve: The highest level of consciousness, encompassing the entirety of existence, the twelfth dimension (12D) represents the ultimate realization of oneness with all that is.

The twelfth dimension is populated by beings of ultimate consciousness, cosmic unity, and Divine essence, representing the highest realization of Divine oneness and cosmic harmony. It is the realm of the singular state of oneness with Father/Mother/God/Prime Source/Creator Consciousness (Source). It is the state of complete and absolute unity, transcending all previous dimensions of consciousness.

These descriptions offer a glimpse into the diverse energies and inhabitants associated with each dimension, showcasing the vastness and complexity of the spiritual and metaphysical realms. As we journey through these dimensions, we gain a deeper understanding of our place in the cosmos and our potential for spiritual evolution.

DENSITIES: DECODING THE LAYERS

Densities refer to the vibrational frequency of mass and the stages of consciousness and spiritual evolution. Each density signifies a different level of awareness and vibrational frequency, with beings evolving through these stages as they progress spiritually.

Mentioned throughout religious texts worldwide, densities form the stepping stones of our cosmic passage. Here is a brief overview of the densities and their significance in spiritual development.

Density One: The most rudimentary density includes elements such as minerals, water, sand, molecules, and electricity. This is the lowest density, corresponding to subatomic particles, atoms, and molecules, where conscious development is basic and limited to simple awareness. Etheric in nature, the first density level encompasses the atomic and subatomic and forms the fundamental particles that make up the basic building blocks of life.

Density Two: This is the place of the unfolding of the seed of life. It is associated with the beginning of carbon based life, such as single-cell organisms, plants, simple organisms, and elemental beings like nature spirits and devas. The second density represents instinctive behavior and basic survival instincts. The second density level lives in the moment and is where consciousness first experiences will, passion, drive, pain, or pleasure.

Density Three: This density includes carbon-based beings, like us, who possess the seed of self-awareness and free will through physical reality and the five senses. Third density serves as a school for learning and spiritual evolution, offering opportunities for growth through challenges and experiences. Third density individuals are often characterized by attachments to material possessions, social status, and physical experiences.

Dimensions one, two, and three are in the third density, and this is called Harmonic Universe One (HU1).

Density Four: Accelerated spiritual growth takes place here and it is where the soul begins to explore the mastery of love. When the physical moves into the fourth density, beings and their environments are part physical and part ethereal. Here we move into the carbon-silica based life forms that straddle the boundary between space-time and the higher ethereal realms.

This realm transcends physical limitations and is associated with the astral plane and non-physical phenomena such as dreams, emotions, and psychic experiences. It is populated by astral beings, spirits, and entities existing beyond the physical realm, including guides, guardians, and departed souls navigating the astral plane.

Density Five: Representing higher consciousness and expanded awareness, the fifth density is often described as a state of unity and interconnectedness transcending duality and separation. It is inhabited by beings of higher consciousness, ascended masters, and light beings, and is often associated with angelic realms and spiritual guides.

The fifth density is where souls begin to explore the mastery of instant manifestation and the wisdom of the light. Beings in this density still possess a body, but it vibrates at a much higher level, making it impossible for the lower densities to see it.

Density Six: Being the realm of archetypal patterns, cosmic laws, and Divine intelligence, the sixth density is associated with higher mental faculties, intuition, and spiritual guidance. It is populated by archetypal energies, cosmic intelligences, and Divine principles, including higher-dimensional beings guiding evolution and spiritual development. This realm is where the soul achieves the mastery of love and light combined. Beings here operate outside of time and space. It is the last density of the physical incarnation cycle.

Dimensions four, five, and six are in Harmonic Universe Two (HU2).

Density Seven: This is a density of spiritual realization and enlightenment and represents the merging of individual consciousness with other consciousness. It is inhabited by enlightened beings, ascended masters, and embodiments of universal consciousness, representing unity and oneness with the Divine. Beings in the seventh density realm are purely non-physical or etheric in nature. They begin to connect with other souls, soul family and soul group members, and begin to experiment with merging consciousness. Life here is silica-crystalline based and at the end of this density cycle, consciousness can be placed in planets and moons and become planetary consciousness.

Density Eight: Beyond human comprehension, the eighth density is often described as the realm of Divine consciousness and cosmic unity. It is associated with the realization of one's true nature as a Divine being. The eighth density is populated by cosmic deities, celestial beings, and Divine manifestations. If souls choose, this density can be where their expanded consciousness can begin to merge with the stars.

Density Nine: The dimension of cosmic harmony and Divine order, the ninth density represents the integration of all aspects of existence into a unified whole. It is inhabited by beings of cosmic harmony, Divine order, and universal balance, including cosmic architects and overseers of universal laws. This is the place of galactic consciousness.

Dimensions seven, eight, and nine are in Harmonic Universe Three (HU3).

Density Ten: A realm of infinite possibilities and potentiality, the tenth dimension is associated with the manifestation of intentions and the co-creation of reality. It is populated by beings of infinite potentiality, creators, and cosmic architects shaping reality, guiding the manifestation of intentions and the co-creation of universes. This is the place where multiple galactic consciousnesses can merge to form galaxies. Beings in this state of pure consciousness or pure crystalline liquid light have returned to their pre-matter states of consciousness.

Density Eleven: Known as the universal template, this is where consciousness comprises the entire universe and a cycle is completed. It holds the laws of the universe, the harmonics, creator councils, archangels, and Elohim geometries. Beyond linear time and space, the eleventh density represents the totality of all possible timelines and realities. It is associated with the concept of parallel universes and multidimensional existence, inhabited by beings who oversee the multiverse and parallel realities.

Density Twelve: This is the realm of the Prime Source/Creator. The highest individuated level of consciousness, encompassing the entirety of existence, the twelfth dimension represents the ultimate realization of oneness with all that is. It is populated by beings of ultimate consciousness, cosmic unity, and Divine essence, representing the highest realization of cosmic harmony. Here the templates of creation are found to contain the building blocks of matter.

Dimensions ten, eleven, and twelve are in Harmonic Universe Four. (HU4)

Densities Thirteen through Fifteen: There are three additional densities that pertain to pre-matter states of existence. While I don't have personal knowledge or experience with these realms, I understand them to be associated with what is often referred to as the void or the etheric body of Source. This domain is believed to encompass the realm of all possibilities, representing pure potentiality. It is where the templates for all of creation are in their pre-form states.

HARMONIC UNIVERSES: THE FRAMEWORK OF REALITY

When I discovered the Harmonic Universe concepts of Lisa Renee, Phil Gruber, and Ashayana Deane in 2019, I was thrilled because they echoed some of the same universal information that I carried within me as a walk-in when I incarnated in 1999. Although similar, there may be some slight differences in my presentation below.

Harmonic Universe 1 (HU-1) — D1-3: The initial harmonic universe encompasses dimensions one through three, forming the tangible physical realm familiar to us in our everyday lives. It serves as the starting point for the soul's odyssey, where it interacts with the solid, material aspects of existence. This realm is where human beings reside in carbon-based bodies, navigating life within the confines of a three-dimensional reality. In this first harmonic universe, carbon-based life forms, typical to Earth, are predominant.

Harmonic Universe 2 (HU-2) — D4-6: The second harmonic universe comprises dimensions four, five and six, covering the astral and mental planes discussed in the next chapter. In this realm, consciousness transcends the physical constraints, venturing into emotional and intellectual territories.

This harmonic universe is noted for its astral or emotional landscape and possesses a physical density less than that of HU-1. Inhabitants of this realm often find themselves in a state of transition—either between physical incarnations or as higher-dimensional beings who no longer require a physical form.

The nature of consciousness here is notably more fluid, focusing primarily on emotional and spiritual development. Beings in HU-2, often carbon-silica hybrids, are characterized by their lighter, more energetically adaptable forms.

Harmonic Universe 3 (HU-3) — D7-9: In the third harmonic universe, which spans dimensions seven, eight and nine, the soul progresses into elevated states of spiritual consciousness with a notable reduction in material density.

This domain is conducive to spiritual revelations and deeper connections, which are predominantly featured. HU-3 facilitates more advanced spiritual activities and functions. This universe is characterized as the realm of spiritual awareness, frequently referred to as the *causal plane* or the *soul matrix*.

Beings and consciousness in this sphere operate with minimal reliance on physical manifestations, engaging primarily through interactions of light and energy. They typically exist in a silica-based configuration.

Harmonic Universe 4 (HU-4) — D10-12: The fourth harmonic universe, encompassing dimensions ten, eleven, and twelve, signifies a pinnacle of spiritual development. Souls within this domain achieve a deep integration with Source.

This elevated plane of existence is often described as the monadic plane or oversoul consciousness. Entities residing in HU-4 transcend physical constraints, functioning as embodiments of pure energy or spiritual essence.

In this advanced state, beings manifest as pure energetic or conscious forms in a silica-crystalline structure. This form allows for a more direct flow of light and energy through the body, facilitating spiritual growth and ascension.

Harmonic Universe 5 (HU-5) — Pre-matter D13-15: The fifth harmonic universe, spanning dimensions thirteen, fourteen, and fifteen, goes beyond the conventional time matrix to establish a direct connection with Source. This paramount realm represents the culmination of the soul's journey, in which it achieves final ascension and reunites with the origin of all creation.

Regarded as the domains of the *Christos* or *avatar consciousness*, this universe is characterized by entities that have fully merged with universal consciousness. Beings in this expanse participate actively in the administration and equilibrium of cosmic energies throughout the various dimensions and universes.

Within both the fourth and fifth harmonic universes, entities manifest as pure energy or consciousness in a crystalline-liquid light structure, allowing for a true multidimensional experience. These souls are engaged in significant cosmic operations, orchestrating processes that influence the grand schematic of the cosmos.

This model provides a comprehensive structure for understanding the soul's journey through various levels of existence, each layer offering unique lessons and opportunities for growth. By examining these harmonic universes, we can gain a deeper appreciation of our spiritual evolution and the interconnectedness of all dimensions.

As we conclude our exploration of densities and dimensions, it is crucial to appreciate the intricate tapestry that binds these concepts within the framework of the harmonic universe. Studying densities and dimensions is an expedition into the essence of our existence and the cosmos itself, which can allow us to better understand our place in the universe.

As we move forward in this exploration, we will delve into universal multidimensionality concepts to help us better understand and align with the harmonics of the cosmos.

UNIVERSAL MULTIDIMENSIONALITY

The universe is a mosaic of intricate layers, each playing a critical role in the fabric of reality. This chapter presents the diverse cosmic concepts of planes of existence, timelines, parallel universes and the multiverse—elements that define the nature of our universe's multidimensionality. These components are essential for understanding the environment in which walk-ins, starseeds, and hybrids operate, as their origins and missions are deeply intertwined with these complex, interwoven realities.

Each element contributes a unique pattern to the overarching design of reality. Planes of existence refer to various levels or dimensions, each possessing distinct vibrational frequencies and forms of consciousness. Timelines, on the other hand, represent the sequential paths that realities follow, branching out in numerous potential directions based on choices and events. Parallel universes suggest a vast array of alternate realities coexisting alongside our own, each diverging due to different decision points and circumstances. Finally, the multiverse encapsulates all of these concepts, positing a universe of universes where all possibilities are realized.

Though these components might appear distinct, they are intrinsically connected, reflecting the complex and interconnected nature of existence itself. This interconnectedness suggests that while each dimension, timeline, and universe operate under its own set of rules and realities, they collectively contribute to a singular, grander structure of the cosmos. Thus, they are separate in function and form but unified in their contribution to the whole—a multidimensional mosaic that illustrates the deep unity underlying the apparent diversity of the universe. This unity in diversity underscores the mystical and scientific wonder of the cosmos, offering a holistic view that challenges and expands our understanding of reality.

As we peel back the layers of these elements, we uncover the diverse stages and settings where our souls travel through various forms of growth and learning. Here, we examine how these dimensions of reality not only coexist but interact, influencing the collective journey of consciousness across time and space and paving the way for transformative shifts in collective awareness.

PLANES OF EXISTENCE

The concept of the seven planes of existence is found in many esoteric and spiritual traditions, each with its own interpretation. While the specifics may vary, the general idea is that reality consists of multiple interconnected planes or levels of existence that have their own characteristics and inhabitants. The image to the right is a commonly referenced framework.

Planes of Existence

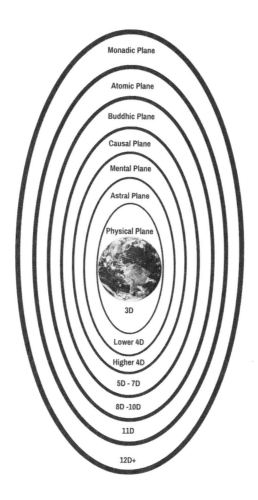

Physical Plane: The physical plane is the level of existence that we are most familiar with, characterized by tangible matter, energy, and the laws of physics. It includes the physical universe, planets, stars, and all material objects. Humans, animals, plants, and all forms of physical life are located here.

Astral Plane: The astral plane is considered a higher-vibrational dimension than the physical. Thoughts, emotions, and psychic phenomena manifest more readily here. This plane is often described as a realm of dreams, imagination, and spiritual experiences beyond the limitations of the physical body.

There are three levels within this plane: the lower astral intersects with the Earth plane or what many call the middle Earth. The middle level is where the halls of learning, the Akashic Records, the halls of records, universal laws, and schools of higher learning are found. The upper level is what most call heaven or paradise. When the soul departs the physical body, it travels through each level. Located within this plane are the astral bodies of the deceased, astral projections of the living, and various astral creatures.

Mental Plane: The mental plane is the realm of pure thought and intellect where ideas, concepts, and universal truths originate. It is where consciousness operates at a higher level of clarity and understanding, transcending the limitations of the physical and astral planes. Higher spiritual beings reside here, as well as advanced souls and the mental forms of enlightened individuals.

Causal Plane: The causal plane is the realm of causality and the source of all creation. It is believed to be the realm where Divine consciousness or cosmic intelligence resides and where the seeds of karma and destiny are sown. Within the causal plane, beings may gain insight into the purpose of existence and the interconnectedness of all things. Those that live within this plane include etheric doubles of living creatures, nature spirits, and elemental beings like fairies and gnomes.

Buddhic Plane: The buddhic plane is associated with pure love, compassion, and spiritual enlightenment. It is considered a realm of heightened awareness and union with the Divine, where beings experience unconditional love and oneness with all creation. Buddhas, bodhisattvas, advanced spiritual masters, devas or celestial beings, and angels or archangels exist on this plane.

Atomic Plane: The atomic plane is the level of existence where individual consciousness merges with universal consciousness, transcending all distinctions and separations. It is a realm of pure beingness and spiritual realization where the ultimate truth is realized beyond all concepts and limitations.

Monadic Plane: The monadic plane is the highest level of existence, often described as the realm of the Divine or absolute reality. It is the source from which all other planes emanate and where the pure essence of existence is experienced in its fullest expression.

The soul is believed to ascend through these planes, gaining wisdom and understanding as it progresses toward unity with the Divine. These seven planes are sometimes depicted as a ladder or staircase with each plane representing a higher level of consciousness and spiritual evolution.

When applying this concept to walk-ins, starseeds, and hybrids, we begin to understand the intricate complexity and purpose of their experiences and roles within the vast cosmic play. This exploration into the structure of our universe's planes reveals a rich, interdimensional ecosystem in which these souls operate and begin to navigate as they descend in their frequency to enter an Earth body. Each plane offers unique challenges and opportunities, encouraging growth and the eventual evolution toward ultimate unity.

By understanding the relationships between these planes and the entities that traverse them, we gain deeper insights into the nature of our universe and our place within it. As we continue to explore and interact with these dimensions, we may find that our own paths of spiritual development are intricately linked to the universal journey toward enlightenment and unity. This realization opens new pathways for personal and collective transformation, heralding a future where the boundaries of existence are expanded by our growing understanding of the multidimensional universe.

TIMELINES

As we delve deeper into the dynamics of timelines, it becomes increasingly clear how pivotal the roles of walk-ins, starseeds, and hybrids are in the grand scheme of cosmic evolution. These beings, each arriving from or awakened to their unique origins and purposes, carry with them not only the potential to elevate human consciousness but also the power to significantly shift timelines.

Walk-in souls that enter a human body and replace the original soul typically arrive during a period of intense personal crisis or a pivotal moment of transformation. Their arrival can catalyze profound changes, not only in their immediate environment but potentially on a much broader scale. The infusion of a new soul with different objectives and higher vibrational energies can reset the trajectory of the host's life path, thereby altering the timeline they were originally on. This change can ripple outward, affecting the collective experience and shifting the potential outcomes of events on a global scale.

Starseeds, imbued with knowledge and energies from distant dimensions, awaken to their mission gradually or through significant life events that serve as catalysts for their spiritual awakening. As they become conscious of their origins and purposes, their elevated vibrations and advanced spiritual understandings can act as transformative agents for their surroundings. If a starseed fully activates their potential, they can initiate a tipping point in consciousness that propels a significant timeline shift, steering collective events toward higher outcomes.

Hybrids, who embody the physical and spiritual genes of both human and extraterrestrial entities, serve as bridges between worlds. Their existence is a blend of multiple dimensions and planes of consciousness. As they come into their full awareness and begin to operate in accordance with their hybrid nature, they can merge the best of all the worlds they represent, potentially stabilizing volatile timelines or opening new paths of evolution that were previously inaccessible.

The arrivals of walk-ins, starseeds, and hybrids carry a profound responsibility. Their actions and the energies they introduce or activate can influence the direction of not just their personal timelines but also impact the broader, collective timelines. Each decision and energetic shift they contribute to can lead to potential outcomes ranging from minor changes in personal relationships to significant global transformations.

Given their powerful ability to influence timelines, it is crucial for these souls to be aware of the broader implications of their awakenings and integrations. They must navigate their paths with a deep awareness of the interconnectedness of all actions and their potential ripple effects across timelines and dimensions. This understanding is essential for ensuring that their contributions lead toward positive outcomes and support the evolutionary progress of humanity and the Earth.

By comprehending the intricate relationships between these entities and the universal structure of planes and timelines, we recognize the delicate balance they maintain and the transformative impact they can have on our collective journey toward enlightenment and cosmic unity. This deeper insight underscores the importance of mindful evolution and the responsible wielding of their abilities to alter timelines for the greater good of all.

As we delve deeper into the content of this chapter, we will uncover that the timelines, while they share similarities, also possess distinct nuances that uniquely define them. It is in these subtle differences and minor details that we can discern the individual characteristics that distinguish one type of timeline from another. Through this exploration, we gain a richer understanding of how each timeline contributes its own thread to the intricate tapestry of the universe, making every version of reality significant in its own right. As you read through the timelines below, you may realize that you are experiencing more than one.

Personal and Collective Timelines: On an individual level, people may experience different timelines or trajectories based on their choices, beliefs, and energetic resonance. Similarly, collective timelines can be influenced by the collective consciousness of humanity, resulting in shifts and changes on a larger scale. Again, many people today are operating within these timelines.

Linear Timelines: These are the most conventional type of timelines, where events unfold in a sequential manner from past through present to future. This is the common understanding of time in everyday life and classical physics, where each moment follows the last in a fixed order.

Parallel Timelines: Parallel timelines suggest the existence of multiple, simultaneous timelines that run in parallel to each other. Each one represents a different sequence of events that might have occurred based on different decisions or outcomes at key moments. These are closely related to the concept of parallel universes in quantum mechanics, where each universe represents a different possible history and future.

Divergent Timelines: These timelines branch off from a primary timeline due to significant events or choices, creating an alternate sequence of events. This concept is often explored in science fiction and time-travel stories, where a change in the past creates a new timeline that diverges from the original.

Convergent Timelines: Convergent timelines involve different timelines or sequences of events that eventually merge into a single timeline, resulting in a unified history. This concept is sometimes used in theories of destiny or fate, where despite different paths or choices, the outcomes converge to a single, pre-determined point.

Cyclic Timelines: In some spiritual and philosophical beliefs, timelines are cyclic rather than linear. This involves events recurring in cycles such as the Yugas, cyclical epochs in Hindu cosmology that represent the gradual decline and regeneration of morality, knowledge, and spirituality across four ages: Satya Yuga, Treta Yuga, Dvapara Yuga, and Kali Yuga, and includes the belief in reincarnation or the cyclic universe theory in cosmology. Each cycle may vary slightly, but certain key events reoccur.

Quantum Timelines: These are based on the principles of quantum mechanics, where all potential outcomes of an event exist simultaneously until a measurement or observation causes one outcome to become reality. Quantum timelines are not experienced sequentially but instead are potential states that exist until they are collapsed into a single state.

Ascended Timelines: In spiritual contexts, ascended timelines represent paths that lead to higher spiritual awareness and enlightenment. These timelines are thought to be affected by conscious spiritual practices, the influence of higher-dimensional beings, or significant energetic shifts on Earth or the cosmos. Many people today are operating in such a timeline.

Healing Timelines: These are pathways where healing—whether emotional, physical, or spiritual—occurs. They can be personal or collective and are often sought through various healing modalities, intending to shift from a timeline of trauma or suffering to one of recovery and well-being.

Potential Timelines: These consist of all possible futures that could emerge, based on current conditions and energies. They are not fixed and can change as circumstances and choices evolve. Potential timelines are often the focus in divination and forecasting practices.

Each type of timeline provides a framework for understanding how events unfold and interact across different dimensions of reality, reflecting the diverse ways that time could be perceived and influenced according to various beliefs and theories.

PARALLEL REALITIES

Beyond the realms of our ordinary perception lies a concept both intriguing and elusive: parallel realities. These alternate dimensions, branching off from our own universe, have captivated the human imagination for centuries, serving as fertile ground for speculation, exploration, and philosophical inquiry.

Parallel realities, also known as alternate realities or parallel universes, are constructs that propose the existence of multiple, coexisting versions of reality. Each reality operates according to its own set of physical laws, dimensions, and timelines, diverging from other realities in subtle or profound ways.

According to some interpretations of quantum mechanics, the universe we perceive may be just one of countless parallel realities existing simultaneously. These realities might differ in fundamental aspects such as the arrangement of matter, the progression of time, and the emergence of life forms, offering infinite possibilities and permutations.

The concept of parallel realities has been embraced by various fields of study including physics, cosmology, and philosophy. Physicists and cosmologists theorize about the existence of a *multiverse*, a vast ensemble of parallel universes comprising our cosmic landscape. In the realm of philosophy, parallel realities provoke questions about the nature of reality, consciousness, and the human experience. Philosophers ponder the implications of multiple realities on concepts such as free will, identity, and the nature of existence itself.

While the idea of parallel realities may seem abstract and fantastical, some theories propose mechanisms through which these realities may interact or converge. Concepts such as quantum entanglement, wormholes, and higher-dimensional geometry offer potential pathways for communication or travel between parallel universes.

What we call speculative fiction presents alternative ways of thinking that might involve parallel realities. These serve as fertile ground for storytelling, providing narrative frameworks for exploring themes of identity, choice, and the consequences of our actions. Works of literature, film, and television sometimes depict characters traversing between parallel realities, encountering alternate versions of themselves, and grappling with the implications of their choices. Is this simply storytelling, or is it preparing us for the truth about our universe and the way it operates?

Beyond the realms of science and philosophy, parallel realities also find resonance in mystical and spiritual traditions. Shamans, mystics, and practitioners of esoteric arts speak of traveling between worlds, accessing hidden dimensions, and communing with beings from alternate realities. In the realm of spirituality, parallel realities offer a lens through which we can explore concepts such as interconnectedness, cosmic consciousness, and the nature of the soul. Some spiritual traditions posit the existence of higher realms or planes of existence inhabited by beings of higher consciousness and wisdom.

Parallel realities remain a tantalizing frontier of exploration, inviting us to contemplate the vastness of existence and the boundless possibilities inherent in the multiverse. Whether viewed through the lens of science, philosophy, or spirituality, the concept of parallel realities calls us to expand our horizons, question our assumptions, and embrace the mystery of the unknown.

ALTERNATE UNIVERSES

As we explore the intricate web of parallel realities, each subtly distinct from the other, we begin to see the vastness of possibilities that exist beyond our current understanding. This natural progression asks us to widen our perspective even further, leading us into the fascinating realm of alternate universes. Just as parallel realities offer a multitude of variations within a single universe, the concept of multiple universes, or the multiverse, suggests an even more expansive structure of existence. Now, let us delve into the idea of these alternate universes—each with its own unique laws, dimensions, and realities—to further expand our understanding of the cosmos.

Alternate Universes: These parallel realities diverge from our own at specific points, resulting in alternate timelines where different choices were made or historical events unfolded differently. In these universes, the fabric of reality may be like our own but with notable differences in societal structures, technological advancements, or geopolitical landscapes.

In recent years, there have been discussions surrounding what is called the "Mandela Effect," a phenomenon in which a large group of people remember something differently than the way it is now believed to have occurred. The effect was named after the South African statesman and activist Nelson Mandela. Many people falsely remember Mandela dying in prison in the 1980s, even though he actually passed away in 2013, long after his release. The Mandela Effect is often discussed in the context of collective memory and psychology. Groups of people can develop shared false memories, likely due to the way memories are stored and reconstructed in the brain. Misinformation, misremembering, and the influence of similar memories can all contribute to this effect—but the merging of parallel realities or timelines might be the most obvious answer.

Dimensional Realities: Different dimensional or spatial realities exist alongside our own, often inaccessible to our senses and unreachable by conventional scientific instruments. These dimensions may operate according to different laws of physics or have entirely distinct properties. The higher dimensions described in string theory and the alternate dimensions sometimes discussed in metaphysical frameworks fall into the category of dimensional realities. In string theory, for example, higher spatial dimensions are compacted or folded in ways that are not perceivable by humans.

Dream Realms: Dreams offer a subjective form of parallel reality where individuals experience alternate scenarios, environments, and interactions while in a state of sleep. These dream realms can range from mundane to fantastical, reflecting the subconscious mind's processing of emotions, memories, desires, and the experiences had during astral or out of body experiences.

Virtual Realities: In the realm of technology, virtual realities simulate parallel worlds through immersive digital environments. Users can interact with these simulated worlds by using virtual reality headsets or computer interfaces, experiencing scenarios and environments that might diverge from physical reality.

Spiritual Realms: Within spiritual and metaphysical belief systems, parallel realities may encompass realms inhabited by spiritual beings, entities, or energies. These realms could include the astral plane or other states of existence beyond the physical realm. Individuals may travel in the spiritual realms during meditation, astral projection, or near-death experiences.

Each type of parallel reality offers its own insights into the nature of existence, consciousness, and the interconnectedness of all things. Exploring these diverse realms can expand our understanding of reality and challenge our perceptions of the universe's boundless potentialities. It also can provide insights into how walk-in, starseeds, and hybrids traverse the universe.

THE VERSES

The concept of different verses, like the multiverse or omniverse, arises from both scientific theories and speculative ideas. Below is a breakdown of the most-referenced types.

Universe: The term universe refers to all of space and time and their contents, including planets, stars, galaxies, and all other forms of matter and energy. It is everything that we can observe, measure, and more.

Multiverse: The multiverse theory proposes the existence of multiple universes, each with its own set of physical laws, parameters, and conditions. In this view, our universe is just one of many within a vast multiverse, each universe branching off into different timelines and possibilities. This theory is discussed in cosmology and theoretical physics such as physical laws and fundamental constants.

Omniverse: An omniverse is a collection that includes every imaginable and unimaginable universe, multiverse, and dimension, some of which are not based on the laws of physics as we understand them. The omniverse is a philosophical or speculative concept, often discussed in metaphysics and works of fiction.

Megaverse: A megaverse refers to a collection of many multiverses, each of which might have its own different sets of laws and constants.

These concepts are used to explore and discuss the nature of existence and reality, often stretching beyond current scientific understanding into speculative territories. Each verse represents a different scope and scale of existence, from our observable universe to potentially infinite collections of all possible realities.

As we conclude this chapter, we are left with a greater appreciation for the intricate and interconnected nature of our universe. This chapter has revealed the layers of reality, exploring how different planes of existence intersect and influence each other; how timelines can diverge and converge in a complex dance of possibilities; and how parallel realities expand our understanding of what it means to exist. It has also illuminated the expansive concept of the verse, a cosmic symphony of all that is, was, and could be. Armed with this knowledge, we are better equipped to navigate our own journeys through the cosmos, recognizing that the reality we experience is but one note in an infinite chorus of the universe's grand design.

In the next chapter, we will begin to understand more fully that every choice we make and every belief we hold has the potential to shape not just our destiny, but the fabric of the universe itself.

THE HOLOGRAPHIC FIELDS

According to my collective and healing teams, significant changes in our energetic bodies have occurred. This happened because of the increase of the vibrational frequency of the human body, influences from the photonic belt, heightened solar particle activity, and more. Notably, the emotional and mental bodies have merged, now functioning across varying octaves containing mega-streams of information. This merger reflects a more integrated approach to how we process emotions and thoughts, facilitating a smoother flow and exchange between feeling and cognition.

Additionally, the electromagnetic field that holds together the astral and causal bodies has expanded. This expanded field now includes specific connection points that link directly to the heart, throat, third eye, and crown chakras and the ley lines of the body. These connection points enhance our ability to integrate higher spiritual frequencies and facilitate deeper communication between our physical existence and higher spiritual realms. This transformation supports a more unified and holistic interaction among our energetic centers, promoting greater harmony and spiritual alignment.

Following are the energetic bodies, each representing different layers of our existence that interact and influence our physical, emotional, mental, and spiritual well-being.

Physical Body: The physical body serves as the container for the soul. It consists of blood, bone, tissue, muscle, systems, organs, and glands. This body is the most tangible expression of our being, interacting directly with the material world.

Etheric Template or Body Double: The body closest to the physical is the etheric body or etheric double. It consists of two parts: the body double and the aura. The etheric body double extends out from and surrounds the physical body by approximately one inch in all directions. It can be seen by some as a golden light.

Composed of fourth-density material, this body carries the blueprint or matrix for the third-density physical body, determining the health and vitality of the physical tissues and organs. This is where the energetic system of the chakras and meridians are located, which energizes and feeds life force energy (*ki, chi,* or *prana*) to the physical systems. The etheric double extends into and energetically attaches within the physical body. The aura, the second part of the etheric body, extends an arm's length around the body in all directions and can be seen by some as a luminescent egg shape, acting as the container for all the subtle bodies.

Emotional/Mental Body: This second body, the emotional body, houses emotional patterns, feelings, and self-esteem. It determines how we interact with ourselves and others, with its vibrations impacting the color and movement of energy seen within the aura. According to my collective, due to the influx of light codes and photonic frequencies that have washed through humanity over the last decades, the electromagnetic field that binds the emotional and mental bodies together has disintegrated merging the two bodies into one. The lowest octave of this body, the emotional body, resides closest to the etheric body. As the vibrations of emotions increase, it ascends into the lowest octave of the mental field.

Mental Body: The higher octave of the second body contains patterns for our thoughts and belief systems. It vibrates between fourth and fifth densities.

Astral Body: The astral body extends eight to twelve inches from the physical body and acts as a portal to the astral and spiritual realm experiences, facilitating astral travel and out-of-body experiences (OBE). It can co-mingle with the auras of others to receive messages and information.

Spiritual Body: This body enables connection to past-life experiences and access to the Akashic Records, holding the patterns needed for spiritual awakening. When aligned and balanced with the other bodies, the spiritual body facilitates a spiritual awakening or quickening, connecting us to higher astral realms.

Celestial Body: The celestial body receives and moderates high vibrational frequencies from universal spiritual realms, integrating these into the spiritual body. This process can elevate consciousness and induce feelings of euphoria and oneness. The celestial body supports the transition from our physical body to our light body and elevates the individual's consciousness and spiritual awareness. It extends about three feet around the physical body.

Crystalline Body: The crystalline body is linked to a state of high vibration. It symbolizes a purified and refined aspect of the subtle body, embodying clarity and elevated consciousness. It connects us to higher dimensional aspects of our energy field or subtle body, representing a state of spiritual purity and high vibration.

THE CHAKRAS

The chakras, referred to as energy vortexes by my collective, are fundamental energy centers within the human body. They play a critical role in spiritual, holistic, and metaphysical practices, especially within traditions like yoga and Ayurveda. These vortexes regulate the flow of energy throughout the body and are pivotal in maintaining balance across physical, emotional, and spiritual dimensions.

Chakras are generally located within the subtle body, which encompasses several layers of energy that are not physical and tangible. The most relevant energetic bodies for the placement and function of the chakras are the etheric body and the astral body.

Chakras

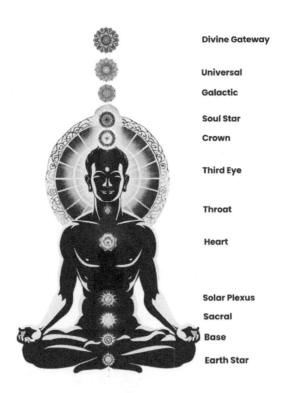

Divine Gateway

Universal

Galactic

Soul Star

Crown

Third Eye

Throat

Heart

Solar Plexus

Sacral

Base

Earth Star

Below is a brief overview of the chakras and their associated attributes:

Divine Gateway Chakra: As the apex of the expanded chakra system, this chakra is located about three feet above the crown chakra and is a direct link to Source energy. It opens the door to ultimate spiritual illumination, connecting you to the infinite realm of Divine creation. By activating this chakra, one can access pure Divine will, infinite consciousness, and the flow of ascended energies. It heralds the peak of spiritual enlightenment and unity with the Divine essence, providing the highest understanding of universal truths and spiritual connection.

Universal Chakra: Resting six inches above the galactic chakra, the universal chakra connects you to the boundless energy of the cosmos. It serves as a conduit to the universal matrix, transcending personal identity and merging with the fabric of the entire universe. This energy center strengthens unity consciousness, infuses universal love, and aligns with cosmic principles. It is a channel for manifesting soul-driven goals that resonate with the greater collective.

Galactic Chakra: Positioned about twelve inches above the soul star chakra, the galactic chakra acts as a bridge to extraterrestrial dimensions, cosmic frequencies, and the wisdom of star civilizations. This chakra is key to awakening starseed consciousness and expanding one's understanding of multidimensional existence. Activating it enhances access to galactic guidance, light codes, and higher frequencies from the universe beyond our solar system.

Soul Star Chakra: Also known as the Gateway of the Soul or the eighth energy center, the soul star chakra is situated approximately six to twelve inches above the crown chakra. This chakra is a portal to Divine wisdom, overseeing spiritual awakening and the integration of higher consciousness. It serves as a reservoir for accessing past-life insights, the Akashic records, and karmic imprints. Through this chakra, one can align with their soul's higher path and unlock deep spiritual potential.

Crown Chakra (Sahasrara): Located at the top of the head and associated with the color violet or white, this chakra connects individuals to higher states of consciousness and the Divine. A balanced crown chakra helps in reaching spiritual enlightenment and feeling a deeper connection to the universe.

Third Eye Chakra (Ajna): Found in the forehead, between the eyebrows, the third-eye chakra is associated with the color indigo. This chakra relates to intuition, foresight, and mental clarity. When open, it facilitates insight and the ability to see beyond the physical.

Throat Chakra (Vishuddha): Situated in the throat and linked with the color blue, this chakra governs communication and expression. A balanced throat chakra enables clear communication and the ability to speak one's truth.

Heart Chakra (Anahata): Located in the center of the chest, this chakra is associated with the color green (or pink). It influences love, compassion, and emotional balance. An open heart chakra allows individuals to form emotional connections with others.

Solar Plexus Chakra (Manipura): Found in the stomach area, this chakra is yellow and controls personal power, self-esteem, and confidence. When in balance, it contributes to a strong sense of self-worth and the power of choice.

Sacral Chakra (Svadhishthana): Positioned just below the navel, this chakra is associated with the color orange. It relates to creativity, sexual energy, and emotional expression. A balanced sacral chakra enhances personal expression and the ability to experience pleasure.

Root Chakra (Muladhara): Located at the base of the spine, this chakra is associated with the color red. It governs survival instincts, security, and basic human necessities. When balanced, it promotes feelings of safety and grounding.

Earth Star Chakra: Located approximately six to twelve inches below the feet, this energy center is associated with grounding and connection to the Earth. It governs our connection to the Earth, the physical plane, and the collective consciousness of humanity. It grounds us into the Earth's core. When balanced, it helps to ground excess energies, supports stability, and strengthens our connection to the planet and universal life force, allowing for deeper alignment with spiritual purpose and earthly presence.

Each chakra is believed to be a nexus of life energy, or prana. The proper function of each chakra is vital for maintaining physical, emotional, and spiritual health. Techniques like meditation, yoga, Reiki, and aromatherapy are often used to balance and align these chakras, promoting overall well-being.

THE MERIDIANS

Meridians, in traditional Chinese medicine, are pathways in the body through which the life-energy known as *qi* flows. Each meridian corresponds to a specific organ or group of organs, promoting a flow of energy that maintains balance, health, and vitality. Below is a brief overview of the major meridians in the body.

Lung Meridian: This meridian regulates the respiratory system and influences the immune system. It starts in the chest, travels down the arm, and ends at the thumb.

Large Intestine Meridian: Responsible for absorption and the excretion process, it starts at the index finger, runs up the arm, and ends at the nose, reflecting its role in clearing waste from the body.

Stomach Meridian: This pathway begins at the face, descends to cover the throat and stomach, and ends at the feet. It influences digestion and general energy levels.

Spleen Meridian: Starting at the big toe, it runs up the leg and body, ending at the chest. This meridian supports the spleen and stomach, impacts digestion, and governs the management of blood cells.

Heart Meridian: It starts in the heart, travels along the arm, and ends at the little finger. The heart meridian governs blood circulation and influences emotional well-being.

Small Intestine Meridian: This meridian begins at the little finger, moves up the arm, and connects to the face. It is involved in digestion, absorption, and the distribution of nutrients along with separating the clear from the turbid in digestion.

Bladder Meridian: The longest meridian, it starts at the inner eye, travels over the head, down the back, along the back of the legs, and ends at the little toe. It governs the urinary bladder and the storage and excretion of urine.

Kidney Meridian: Beginning at the foot, this pathway travels up the body, ending in the chest. The kidney meridian is crucial for urinary health, reproduction, and the body's vital energy.

Pericardium Meridian: This meridian runs from the chest along the middle of the arm and ends at the tip of the middle finger. It protects the heart and regulates the circulatory system.

San Jiao Meridian: Commonly known as the Triple Burner, this meridian starts at the ring finger, passes through the arm and ends at the eyebrow. This meridian helps regulate the three energy centers of the body—upper, middle, and lower—managing the movement of water and heat.

Gallbladder Meridian: Beginning at the outer corner of the eye, this meridian zigzags across the side of the body, ending at the fourth toe. It is involved in decision-making and the health of the gallbladder.

Liver Meridian: Starting at the big toe, this pathway runs up the leg and ends at the chest. It regulates the liver functions, affecting detoxification, the quality of blood, and emotional balance.

Each meridian plays a vital role in maintaining the health and harmony of the corresponding organs and bodily functions, illustrating the holistic view of health in traditional Chinese medicine. Meridians are holographic in nature and serve as pathways for health and vitality.

LEY LINES

Ley lines represent a powerful connection between our bodies and the universe. These lines aren't just pathways within us; they are energy streams of data that connect us to the broader cosmos. This connection allows for an exchange of spiritual and energetic frequencies that influence our daily lives.

Each ley line interacts with specific areas in our bodies and universal energies that influence our spiritual journey and growth. Through these connections, we see how our physical, energetic, and spiritual worlds are intertwined, helping us to better understand our place within the cosmos.

Ley lines traverse multiple dimensions. They run left to right and front to back, enveloping the physical connection points in a lattice that echoes the sacred geometries of the universe. This concept might resonate with the

Indigenous peoples' understanding of the web of life, suggesting a universal grid or network that sustains all existence, not confined to the individual but expansive, connecting all life forms in a profound symbiosis.

Each ley line corresponds to a different aspect of human and cosmic existence, manifesting through various energy centers or matrices and contributing to our spiritual evolution. Each of these bodies is intricately linked through ley lines, forming a holistic system that reflects the complex interplay between the physical, energetic, spiritual, and multidimensional aspects of existence. They depict a sophisticated understanding of how energies interact within and beyond the human experience, highlighting a layered approach to spiritual evolution and consciousness expansion.

These holographic grid structures were revealed to me by my collective. I have used them successfully in my practice with thousands of clients and the students that I have taught. I call this information Soul Reconnection Technique.

Ley Lines &
Spiritual Body Association

Ley Line Twelve	Crystalline Shield
Ley Line Eleven	Crystalline Body
Ley Line Ten	Celestial Body
Ley Line Nine	Spiritual Body
Ley Line Eight	Crown Matrix
Ley Line Seven	Third Eye Matrix
Ley Line Six	Throat Matrix
Ley Line Five	Heart Matrix
Ley Line Four	Astral Body
Ley Line Three	Emotional/Mental Body
Ley Line Two	Etheric Body
Ley Line One	Physical Body

There is so much more to each ley line than I list, but a summary should give you a basic understanding of the complexities of each. Next is an overview of the twelve ley lines.

Physical Ley Line:

Function: Connects to the iron core of Mother Earth. It is grounding and provides physical structure.

Location: This ley line runs across and beneath the feet.

Related Energy Center: Earth Star

Emotion: Influences feelings like fear and depression, grounding trauma.

Etheric Ley Line:

Function: Carries original soul codes and unfolds the soul's plan for this life found in the crystalline core of the Earth.

Location: This ley line rests across the hips.

Related Energy Center: Root, which surrounds the body.

Emotion: Addresses lack of trust and fight-or-flight patterns.

Emotional/Mental Ley Line:

Function: Carries personal soul codes, influencing emotional and mental experiences.

Location: Across the belly button.

Related Energy Center: Sacral

Emotion: Related to creativity, sense of worth, and relationship issues.

Astral Ley Line:

Function: Acts as a barrier, providing protection and stability.

Location: Across the solar plexus or diaphragm area.

Related Energy Center: Solar plexus

Emotion: Deals with negativity and external opinions impacting self-esteem.

Heart Matrix Ley Line:

Function: Balances masculine and feminine energies, facilitating transformation.

Location: The matrix field is home of the Heart Matrix ley line. It extends from the field and connects to the heart and out into the cosmos.

Related Energy Center: Heart

Emotion: Concerns deep-seated childhood and adult hurts.

Throat Matrix Ley Line:

Function: Focuses on manifestation and the expression of truth.

Location: From the matrix field to the throat and into the cosmos.

Related Energy Center: Throat

Emotion: Addresses issues like indecisiveness and repressed emotions.

Third Eye Matrix Ley Line:

Function: Connects to stargates and multidimensional selves.

Location: From the matrix field to the third eye and out to the cosmos.

Related Energy Center: Third eye

Emotion: Involves self-doubt and issues with control.

Crown Matrix Ley Line:

Function: Distributes universal energies and fosters unity consciousness.

Location: Across the top of the head.

Related Energy Center: Crown

Emotion: Concerns overthinking and rigidity.

Spiritual Body Ley Line:

Function: Connects with the blueprints of creation and karmic cycles.

Location: The spiritual body extends approximately 18" – 24" from and around the body.

Related Energy Center: Soul Star

Emotion: Positioned beyond emotional disturbances.

Celestial Body Ley Line:

Function: Connects with Divine love and higher collective plans.

Location: The celestial body extends approximately 24" – 36" from and around the body.

Related Energy Center: Galactic

Emotion: Beyond typical emotional entanglements.

Crystalline Body Ley Line:

Function: Connects with Christ consciousness and higher universal consciousness fields.

Location: The crystalline body extends approximately 36" – 48" from and around the body.

Related Energy Center: Universal

Emotion: Elevated above typical human emotional responses.

Crystalline Shield Ley Line:

Function: Represents the ultimate connection to Source and the morphogenic fields of pre-matter.

Location: This shield adheres to the crystalline body and can extend away from the body as far as 72".

Related Energy Center: Divine Gateway

Emotion: Transcends typical emotional states.

These ley lines facilitate personal growth and spiritual awakening and connect everyone to broader cosmic energies and consciousness. They represent a sophisticated and esoteric understanding of how human energy fields interact with universal forces, reflecting deep spiritual beliefs and practices.

Overall, ley lines not only amplify psychic and spiritual abilities but also serve as meeting points for all beings, creating networks where they can connect, share experiences, and support each other in their spiritual journeys on Earth.

THE MATRIX FIELDS

These fields are a network of multidimensional energies that extends from the body along the ley lines into the cosmos, creating a seamless link between the individual and the vast expanse of the universe. Streams of energy connect to, surround, and extend from the heart, throat, third eye, and crown to higher cosmic and multidimensional frequencies. These matrices are connected to each of the below locations and extend well beyond the confines of the holographic field.

Heart Matrix: The heart chakra is central to our ability to love unconditionally. This field refers to a concept that combines elements of multidimensionality, including both the physiological and energetic perspectives of the body. The heart matrix is considered a complex network of electromagnetic fields and energies centered around the heart. It is crucial for the overall bioenergetic health of the body. This concept is often discussed in alternative medicine and metaphysical frameworks, as well as in some interpretations of heart-brain interactions from a more scientific standpoint.

The heart matrix field can be visualized as an intricate web of electromagnetic and energetic pathways that radiate outward from the heart. Scientifically, the heart generates the strongest electromagnetic field in the body, measured to be about sixty times greater in amplitude than the brain waves recorded in an EEG. This field extends several feet from the body and can be detected and measured by sensitive instruments.

The heart matrix field is often depicted as a luminous, expansive energy field that not only surrounds but also penetrates the body, linking the physical heart to higher states of consciousness and emotional processing capabilities. It might be visualized as a radiant aura or a series of intricate light patterns that continuously interact with and adapt to both internal physiological processes and external environmental energies.

Throat Matrix: Centered around the throat, this matrix field is pivotal for communication, creative expression, and manifestation. It appears in the shape of an electromagnetic box connecting to the throat and extending along the ley line into the original time/space matrix, providing insight into its broader implications and powers, particularly in terms of manifestation, by disconnecting from the concepts of the false matrix.

Third-Eye Matrix: Positioned between the eyebrows, it governs intuition and awareness and acts as a gateway between the physical world and the higher spiritual realms. The third-eye matrix facilitates the transition of energy and information between these dimensions, helping to bring higher dimensional knowledge and wisdom into conscious awareness by connecting us to our multidimensional selves and the collective consciousness.

Crown Matrix: Situated at the top of the head, the crown matrix is the energetic epicenter of Divine energy intake and spiritual communication. It connects an individual to the universe's vast and boundless dimensions, facilitating the flow of cosmic energy into the physical and subtle bodies. This matrix helps in integrating all the lower chakra energies with the higher spiritual energies. It balances the inner spiritual journey with the outer physical life, helping individuals live in a state of heightened awareness and harmony with the cosmos.

THE AURA

The aura, as described within the context of energetic spiritual bodies, is a multidimensional energy field container that surrounds and permeates the physical and spiritual bodies and the matrix fields. It is not a single entity but a complex system of layers that interact with and represent different aspects of an individual's physical, emotional, mental, and spiritual health. It has a crystalline shell that serves to shield the exterior and helps to modulate the influx of higher dimensional energies.

Additionally, the spiritual bodies are all connected within the aura via the human holographic field, which integrates with the energetic field surrounding the physical body, as a complex, dynamic system that encodes and processes information in a holistic, multidimensional manner.

Composition and Layers: The aura is often visualized as a luminous body that extends around the physical body, typically seen as an egg-shaped field of various colors and layers. Each layer of the aura corresponds to the different energetic bodies:

- Closest to the physical body, the etheric layer (related to the etheric body) reflects physical health and vitality.
- The emotional/mental layer shows emotional changes, thoughts, and mental processes.
- Matrix fields connect the heart, throat, third eye, crown chakra, and ley lines to higher multidimensional frequencies.
- Further out, the astral layer allows us to traverse time and space.
- Causal bodies, encompassing the spiritual, celestial, and crystalline bodies, serve as conduits to higher dimensional energies, moderating these energies before they integrate with the physical body.
- The holographic grid permeates the entirety of the auric field.

The aura acts as a container for all the subtle bodies and it plays a crucial role in interacting with the environment. It absorbs and transmits energy from and to the surroundings, influencing and being influenced by the energies around it. The aura is also reflective of the psychological and spiritual states, with its colors and clarity providing insight into one's well-being and spiritual evolution.

Variations in the aura's colors, brightness, and clarity can indicate physical, emotional, or spiritual distress. Practitioners of various holistic and energetic therapies often assess the aura to diagnose imbalances before they manifest as physical ailments.

Understanding the aura as a holographic field enhances approaches to spiritual and energetic healing. Practitioners might focus on altering vibrational patterns within the aura to affect healing, rather than addressing physical symptoms alone. Techniques such as Soul Reconnection Technique™ and Holographic Grid Realignment—both techniques were channeled to me by my collective— as well as Reiki, acupuncture, and other forms of energy work aim to manipulate the holographic patterns to restore balance and health.

In light of recent shifts due to increased cosmic energies, the aura has adapted by expanding its electromagnetic shield and incorporating connection points that align with major chakras like the heart, throat, third eye, and crown. These adaptations help integrate higher vibrational energies and enhance spiritual communication.

The aura, therefore, serves as a dynamic interface between an individual and the broader cosmos, reflecting the interplay of all energetic bodies and external influences, adjusting and evolving in response to spiritual growth and environmental changes.

THE HOLOGRAPHIC GRID

The holographic grid system, woven throughout the aura, look like a piece of grid paper with electric streams of light moving horizontally and vertically. It is located just beneath and through the whole of the aura. It is a complete data set of information about an individual's life force, emotions, thoughts, spiritual well-being, and potential futures. This means that every fragment of the holographic field can reveal comprehensive insights about the entire being, if we consider that the aura is actually a holographic grid.

The holographic grid of the human body is a complex, multi-dimensional framework that encapsulates the entire human being—physically, energetically, and spiritually. It is made up of light and energy patterns that function like a blueprint for the physical body. It extends beyond the visible and tangible, intersecting with the body's energetic layers (or aura) and connecting with the chakras, meridians, and ley lines. This grid is not static; it dynamically responds to internal and external stimuli, reflecting changes in emotional, mental, and spiritual states.

The grid stores vast amounts of personal and universal information, much like a cosmic database. This includes past experiences, genetic information, emotional memories, and spiritual insights. It holds ancestral influences, miasmic imprints, ancestral curses, old contracts, karmic blockages, behavioral patterns, past-life traumas, soul wounds, and more from this or any other lifetime, dimension, or timeline. It operates similarly to the concept of the Akashic Records, where every thought, action, and event is recorded—except in this case, the information is imprinted into the field.

The grid acts as a template from which the etheric template or body double gathers its information to manifest the physical body. According to holographic universe theories, the physical world is a projection of informational patterns. The body's health and condition, therefore, are directly influenced by the information and energy patterns held within this grid.

The grid also links an individual's consciousness to the broader cosmic framework, facilitating exchanges of energy and information. This connection is key to understanding the interdependence of all things within the universe.

By interacting with this grid, practitioners of energy healing modalities such as Reiki, Qi gong, and others can not only affect changes on a physical level but also adjust the energetic and informational patterns that underlie health and consciousness.

The holographic field can store vast amounts of experiential and emotional memories. Each experience an individual goes through imprints itself in the holographic field, influencing the person's energetic presentation and interactions with the environment.

My collective showed me that, instead of thinking of cells of the body as individual cells, I should think of them as microchips that can contain information as far back as the individuation of the soul from the original Source.

The holographic grid's nature allows it to function as both a receiver and a transmitter of information, enabling a person to project their inner reality into the external world and to absorb external energies into their inner world. This reciprocal action is fundamental to how individuals perceive reality and interact with their surroundings.

The human holographic grid presents an expansive view of human existence. It aligns with many spiritual traditions that see the human being as a reflection of the cosmos, deeply interconnected and infinitely complex.

CHANGES TO THE HOLOGRAPHIC FIELD

When a walk-in, starseed, or hybrid arrives or awakens, it causes changes not just in consciousness but also in the holographic structures of the individual. Below, I explain how human spiritual bodies, auras, and holographic grids are affected and consequently need to adapt during such transformative experiences.

The incoming soul carries a different vibrational frequency that is much higher than the original soul prior to arrival or awakening. It has its own set of life purposes, necessitating a substantial reconfiguration of the aura and holographic grid's energetic framework. This adjustment aligns the physical and energetic bodies with the new soul's past experiences, karmic patterns, and spiritual missions. This transition usually occurs over a period of time, but sometimes it is quicker and causes the host to become ill, disconnected, and confused.

The chakra system, meridians, and ley lines undergo realignment to better serve the new soul's energy requirements and spiritual tasks. This realignment can manifest as physical symptoms, emotional upheavals, or profound shifts in consciousness.

Dormant codes within their DNA and energetic bodies become activated, enhancing their spiritual abilities and aligning them more closely with their cosmic origins. This activation can expand their aura and refine the holographic grid to embody higher-dimensional frequencies. It can activate healing abilities, the clairs, past-life memories, galactic memories, spiritual talents, and memories that were not originally accessible.

The awakening leads to an expansion of consciousness, which can significantly alter the structure and function of their spiritual bodies. The aura might exhibit new colors, and the energetic vibration can rise markedly, facilitating deeper connections to higher dimensional beings and energies.

The synthesis of diverse energetic and spiritual attributes requires a recalibrated energetic field that supports their complex nature. This involves the creation of new energetic pathways or the modification of existing ones to accommodate the new frequencies, unique capacities and roles.

Individuals may experience heightened sensitivity and enhanced psychic abilities as their spiritual bodies adjust. They might need to use grounding techniques and energetic protection strategies to manage the intensified perceptions. Regular energetic clearing and healing become crucial to maintain balance and harmony within the spiritual bodies as they adjust to new frequencies and realities.

Profound transformations in the aura and holographic grid often lead to significant shifts in self-identity, life purposes, and existential perspectives, requiring personal adjustments and sometimes external guidance. These transformative experiences emphasize the fluid and dynamic nature of our spiritual structures, adapting not only to earthly life but also to the broader cosmos, embodying changes that facilitate spiritual evolution and fulfillment of soul missions.

OUR JOURNEY AHEAD

Understanding these beginning chapters provides a crucial foundation as we delve into the realms of walk-ins, starseeds, and hybrids. These concepts not only frame our perception of the universe and physical body but also guide us in navigating the complexities of our spiritual evolution.

In the chapters that follow, we will explore the experiences and insights of those who have journeyed through these realms, providing a deeper understanding of the cosmic convergence that unites us all. In the hypnosis sessions conducted by Barbara Lamb, we will hear from walk-ins who have transitioned from one dimension or density to another; starseeds who have come from distant star systems to aid in humanity's evolution; and hybrids who embody the union of different cosmic lineages.

Each chapter will build upon the knowledge of the previous chapters, offering practical guidance and spiritual wisdom to assist us on our journey of cosmic convergence. We will gain insight into the transformative power of higher consciousness, the challenges and opportunities of multidimensional existence, and the profound interconnectedness that binds us all.

In this grand tapestry of existence, we are all co-creators, weaving our unique threads into the collective fabric of the universe. By understanding and embracing the infinite realms of dimensions and densities, we can navigate our cosmic journey with greater awareness, purpose, and joy.

As we traversed the intricate landscapes of dimensions, densities, and holographic universes, we've explored ways in which reality bends and folds—revealing that time and space are far more malleable and interconnected than previously imagined. These insights lay the groundwork for understanding the existence of beings who transcend traditional earthly bounds. In the next sections, as we hear the personal narratives of walk-ins, starseeds, and hybrids, we can deepen our comprehension of the cosmos and learn of the extraordinary interconnections that link us to the far reaches of the universe, inviting us to reimagine what it means to be human in a multidimensional cosmos.

SECTION ONE
WALK-INS

DANCE OF THE SOUL

I would like to begin this chapter with an overview of what a soul is and how I perceive the incarnation process before discussing its various journeys. The concept of the soul, often regarded as the essence of an individual's being, transcends mere physical existence and encompasses the entirety of one's consciousness and spiritual identity. In my understanding, the soul is an eternal and Divine essence that embarks on a path of self-discovery and evolution across various lifetimes and dimensions. The soul is the essence of our true selves, carrying within it the accumulated wisdom, experiences, and lessons from past incarnations.

The incarnation process, as described by my collective, is the mechanism through which the soul enters the physical realm to experience life in a tangible form. It involves the descent of the soul from higher spiritual realms into a physical body, where it undergoes a multitude of experiences, challenges, and growth opportunities. Each incarnation presents a unique opportunity for the soul to learn, grow, and fulfill its spiritual destiny. Through the incarnation process, the soul navigates the complexities of human existence, striving to align with its Divine purpose and achieve enlightenment and unity with Source.

SOUL INCENSION PROCESS

From the depths of the spiritual realm, the soul emerges into the physical plane as an individuation of the Prime Source Creator. Everything originates from Mother/Father/God/Prime Source/Creator. Source itself is composed of pure consciousness plasma called *source plasmatic consciousness* or *source essence*, which emanates through the whole of everything. Some call this essence the morphogenic field. We are unified with and by this essence and it resides within each of us.

When Source sought to experience itself in diverse manifestations of form, patterns of creation emerged called the templates of creation. These templates are the thought forms of Source. Contained within the templates are the blueprints or archetypal patterns for all forms of existence and experience. They hold the potential for everything and contain the fundamental principles and structures upon which the universe and all its manifestations are built.

The following illustration is intended to provide a visual representation of the various phases of the soul's incension process. It is hard to describe a single point that resonates out and expands as it evolves. For the purposes of understanding the concepts, I have chosen to use a vertical drawing.

The blueprint and the template discussed here, is the one we refer to as the soul. When discussing the soul and it various forms, we're pointing to a singular blueprint present in a template of creation. As this blueprint unfolds, the journey of the soul begins. These blueprints are held within the Source Consciousness Monad.

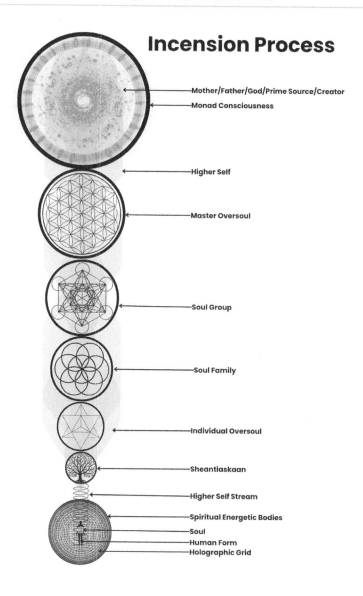

Incension Process

————Mother/Father/God/Prime Source/Creator
————Monad Consciousness

————Higher Self

————Master Oversoul

————Soul Group

————Soul Family

————Individual Oversoul

————Sheantiaskaan

————Higher Self Stream

————Spiritual Energetic Bodies
————Soul
————Human Form
————Holographic Grid

Monad: As described by my collective, the Monad holds all the templates of creations, all the thought forms of Source. Within this framework, the Monad is understood to be the consciousness of Source, meaning it is a dynamic, energetic form that transcends physical limitations and exists on all planes of reality. Some believe the monad to be the *void*–the place of all possibilities.

Higher Self: All variations of the soul emanate from and are contained within the higher self, which represents the highest aspect of the soul directly connected to Source. The higher self is the ultimate Divine container in which all soul existence unfolds. It connects us to every living being and serves as a bridge between the individual self and the Divine. It embodies higher qualities such as wisdom, love, and unity consciousness.

Evolution within this context is viewed as the journey of the soul toward greater alignment with its higher self and, ultimately, with Source. This evolution encompasses experiences of growth, learning, and transformation, all aimed at realizing and actualizing the inherent divinity within.

The higher self is considered by some to be the locus of this evolutionary process. This implies that the higher self is the central point or focal point where the process of soul evolution occurs. It serves as the guiding force for transformation and alignment with Divine essence.

Master Oversoul: The first expression of the soul template is that of the master oversoul. The concept of the master oversoul suggests a foundational essence from which individual souls emerge and evolve. It's akin to a primordial blueprint, the quintessential form from which all other expressions of the soul stem. This oversoul contains the entirety of potential experiences, lessons, and growth that a soul may undergo throughout its existence.

Within the master oversoul, there exists an intricate tapestry of possibilities, each thread representing a unique life experience or incarnation that a soul may undertake. These expressions vary in nature, ranging from moments of joy and triumph to challenges and hardships. Every individual soul emerges from this vast reservoir of potentiality imbued with its own distinct characteristics and purposes.

The master oversoul represents the boundless potential and interconnected nature of the soul's journey. It is the wellspring from which all individual expressions of consciousness emerge, evolve, and ultimately reunite, enriching the universal experience along the way.

Within the master oversoul, the first division of frequencies occur as a natural consequence of the diverse lessons that souls are destined to learn throughout their evolution. These frequencies represent varying levels of consciousness, each resonating with themes, energies, and challenges tailored to the unique growth trajectory of individual souls.

Moreover, the division of frequencies fosters a sense of cosmic order and balance ensuring that every soul encounters the lessons necessary for its growth and the expansion of experiences for Source. Each frequency band serves as a classroom, providing souls with the opportunity to learn, evolve, and ultimately transcend the limitations of their earthly existence.

The division of frequencies within the master oversoul also reflects the inherent intelligence and purpose underlying the soul's journey. It is a sacred dance of consciousness, orchestrated with precision and love, guiding each soul toward its highest potential amidst the vast expanse of the universe.

Soul Groups: At the heart of this division lies the innate wisdom of the universe, organizing souls into vibrational clusters or soul groups based on the lessons they are destined to explore. Some soul groups may resonate with themes of love, compassion, and unity while others might align with concepts of struggle, resilience, and transformation. Each frequency acts as a beacon, attracting souls that are in resonance with its energetic signature.

Soul Families: As souls emerge from the unified essence of the soul group, they not only carry their unique frequency signatures but also begin to gravitate toward others with whom they share resonance and kinship. This natural inclination toward similarity and familiarity leads to the formation of soul families, cohesive groups of souls bound together by shared lessons, purposes, and energetic vibrations.

Within these soul families, souls find solace, support, and understanding as they navigate the complexities of existence. There is a deep sense of alignment and connection as members of the same soul family recognize each other on a soul level, resonating with the familiar frequencies that they share. This recognition often transcends earthly relationships, spanning across lifetimes and dimensions.

Soul families serve as pillars of strength and companionship throughout the soul's journey, providing a sense of belonging and unity amidst the vastness of the universe. Members of a soul family often incarnate together, playing various roles in each other's lives to facilitate growth, healing, and evolution. These soul contracts, forged before incarnation, serve as the framework for the soul's earthly experiences, guiding them toward greater understanding and enlightenment.

Moreover, soul families act as catalysts for spiritual awakening and expansion. They can serve as mirrors through which souls can reflect upon their own growth and evolution. Members of a soul family may incarnate in different roles and circumstances offering diverse perspectives and insights that contribute to the collective learning of the group.

Within the intricate dynamics of soul families exists a profound journey of individuation, wherein each member progresses along their unique evolutionary path toward greater self-awareness and autonomy. As souls undergo evolution within the nurturing embrace of their soul family, they eventually reach a pivotal moment of readiness to embark on their own individual journey of self-discovery.

Primary or Individual Oversoul: The process of individuation marks a significant milestone in the soul's evolution, as it signifies the soul's readiness to step into its own sovereignty and independence, to forge its own path, guided by the wisdom and experiences accumulated through its interactions within the family unit. Each soul family is comprised of individuated souls called primary or individual oversouls.

As the individuating soul integrates more fully within its individual oversoul, it gains access to a higher perspective and expanded consciousness, which enables it to navigate the complexities of existence with grace and clarity. This newfound sense of self-awareness empowers the soul to co-create its reality in alignment with its highest purpose and intentions.

While the path of individuation may lead the soul away from its soul family in a physical sense, the bonds forged within the heart and soul remain eternally intact. Each member of the soul family continues to support and uplift the others on their respective paths, celebrating the unique expressions of divinity that emerge through the process of individuation.

The essence of individuation represents a sacred dance of self-discovery and self-realization wherein each soul embraces its inherent divinity and steps into the fullness of its being. Through this journey, the soul not only honors its connection to its soul family but also celebrates the infinite possibilities of growth and expansion that lie ahead on the path of evolution.

While individual souls may seem separate in their earthly manifestations, they are intrinsically linked to the greater whole through the higher self and Source. This interconnectedness fosters a sense of harmony and collaboration among souls as they navigate their respective paths.

Sheantiaskaan: Within the primary oversoul resides a minimum of twelve *sheantiaskaan*. The sheantiaskaan function as individual vessels through which the *higher-self stream*, spiritual bodies, and soul essence flow. The higher-self stream is an aspect of the higher self that ensures the coherence and alignment of all frequencies contained within. The sheantiaskaan is like the soul's own personal cloud storage, uploading and downloading information and experiences as required. It contains all the memories, events, and feelings that we have ever experienced. Some call the sheantiaskaan the individual oversoul, recognizing the pivotal role in channeling and embodying these deep aspects of existence.

More than one sheantiaskaan can incarnate at a time, thus creating multiple existences in this universe or others; in this dimension or others; on this planet or others. Think of the sheantiaskaan as an octopus. The octopus body represents the primary oversoul and the tentacles are the individual, multidimensional experiences or sheantiaskaan.

When the sheantiaskaan is ready for an incarnation experience, a stream of its energy becomes first the higher self and then the soul. The higher self—our highest Divine expression during a lifetime—remains attached to the sheantiaskaan. It serves as a conduit between us and the sheantiaskaan and acts as a guidance system for us. It is neither affected nor influenced by our experiences during an incarnation, so the information it provides to us remains untainted. As the energy of the higher self becomes denser, it attaches to the physical form. The portion that attaches is called the *soul essence*, or soul, and serves as the personality for the lifetime. When the soul enters the physical body, it does so through the top of the head. It attaches to the body when the first breath is taken and remains attached until the final breath occurs, unless you have a walk-in experience. The soul receives its nourishment and connection to the higher spiritual realms through the spiritual bodies.

SOUL-EXCHANGE WALK-INS

In the vast morphogenic field of existence, one phenomenon that transcends the boundaries of conventional understanding of the soul is the concept of walk-ins. Beyond mere chance or wishful thinking, soul-exchange walk-ins represent a purposeful, acute, and transformative experience wherein the natal or original soul of one person willingly departs, making space for another, more highly evolved soul to inhabit its physical form. The exchange is an intricate, pre-ordained, or sometimes opportunistic dance of the souls.

Unlike traditional births, where the soul enters the body during the birth process and attaches when the baby takes its first breath, walk-ins typically occur later in life. Although they can happen at any time, the soul often enters during moments of severe crisis or chaotic transition. The departing soul (or *walk-out* soul), having completed its mission or facing insurmountable challenges, willingly gives up its earthly existence, making room for the incoming soul to assume its role and take on all its miasmic karmic patterns and unfinished work.

The walk-out's journey does not end with its exit from the physical form. Instead, this soul ascends to higher planes of existence, carrying with it the wisdom and experiences gleaned from its time on Earth. Meanwhile, the incoming soul steps into the vacated body.

Each walk-in brings to this plane of existence its own soul resonant frequency. As the frequency anchors into the physical form, it begins to immediately imprint on the current cellular structure. This infusion brings about an enormous range of physical, mental, and emotional changes. Fortunately, each cell of the body contains its own memory bank capable of storing vast amounts of information from both souls. Unfortunately, the mixed data can present challenges as the cells strive to maintain the highest frequency, pushing the lower frequencies into the emotional body and depositing deep cellular imprints. These imprints must be cleared during the integration phase before the soul can fully anchor its frequency into the body.

During the soul integration phase, karmic, miasmic, ancestral, and/or behavioral patterns emerge as the new, higher frequencies push the old, lower frequencies into the emotional and mental body. This causes an accelerated clearing of the lower frequency patterns. Additionally, the body's holographic toroidal matrix, ley lines, chakras, meridians, and spiritual bodies are each upgraded and, in most cases, the new replaces the original ones. This can be an unsettling and challenging time.

The integrating soul goes through a process to acclimate to the new body and life circumstances. This process can vary in duration and intensity, depending on the compatibility between the incoming soul and the body as well as the level of awareness and preparation of both souls involved. Sometimes a soul will visit their soon-to-be body to begin a slow frequency-imprinting phase. The new soul will observe the day-to-day activities, habits, and customs of its future person. In other cases, the soul will enter and immediately have their spiritual/medical team begin the upgrades. Still others will have these fields switched out over an extended period.

When a walk-in incarnates on Earth, it alters the course of the current timeline and the collective consciousness as it brings and anchors new, higher frequencies and light codes onto the Earth and into the collective consciousness. These frequencies and codes provide help for soul healing, growth, and expansion. They serve as catalysts for deep transformation on both a personal and a planetary scale.

In *Walk-Ins: Cosmology of the Soul,* I shared my personal walk-in experience and recounted the stories of fifteen other people who have experienced the walk-in soul phenomenon. I depicted various categories of walk-ins and delved into their diverse origins. Since then, I have acquired an abundance of additional experiences, knowledge, and encounters, a quantity far beyond anything I could have imagined possible. Even during the writing of this book, two very close friends underwent integration processes of new soul aspects that further broadened my knowledge about the magnitude of the soul and the experiences it seeks to evolve.

In 1999, at the onset of my journey, discussions about walk-ins were virtually nonexistent. There were few resources, minimal literature, and no individuals openly discussing the topic. There was no information on the epigenetics of the soul or even how the incarnation process occurs.

Typically, when a soul aspect or fractal incarnates, it enters the body from a variety of places, including but not limited to a resting place, other planets, different densities, other dimensions, or different realms—or it might reincarnate from a former Earth existence. We will discuss this further in a different section.

When I entered the Sheila body, I expressed myself from my primary, individual, seventh-density oversoul collective—a merged composition of my other multidimensional selves. The main expressions I merged with are the Angelic, Pleiadian, Lyran-Sirian, Arcturian, Mantis, and Andromedan selves. I fondly call this group my collective, as I have embodied each of these aspects and I'm able to call upon them as needed for healing, research, problem-solving, and writing. All I need to do is ask the question and they will answer it.

For those who may be unfamiliar with my soul-exchange walk-in experience, below is a brief overview.

· · · · · · · · · · · · · · ·

In mid to late fall of 1999, a life-changing event altered the course of my life. I was plagued with significant health challenges while navigating a tumultuous marriage, caring for three children, and balancing the demands of a high-profile career.

During the previous twenty years, I had faced diagnoses and suspicions of various ailments including brain tumors, bone cancer, fibromyalgia, chronic fatigue, migraines, multiple sclerosis, sarcoidosis, and erythema nodosum. At times, I relied on a cane to walk, and I had recently been diagnosed with early-stage rheumatoid arthritis. Despite diligently following Western medical advice, I found only limited relief as my symptoms persisted and compounded. This relentless health struggle took a toll on my work, my family, and my overall quality of life as I struggled increasingly to maintain my focus and productivity.

One evening, exhausted, full of despair and in physical pain, I fell into bed. Around seven a.m., it felt as if someone reached down, grabbed me by the hair, and pulled me bolt upright in bed. I felt a sensation like lightning run through my body. Then I was in a space of blinding white light. Despite its suddenness, I liked it. It felt comfortable, familiar, and safe. I was totally at peace and no longer in pain. I don't know how long I was in this space, but slowly, my vision began to return, first at the periphery and then moving toward the center. I looked around the room in a daze. Everything looked the same but felt somehow different. My life at that moment had forever changed.

Suddenly, I remembered past lives that I did not believe in. I remembered ceremonies and Indigenous healing methods that I had never read about, believed, nor expressed an interest in. I had universal truths floating around in my head that I had never studied. I was suddenly clairvoyant, claircognizant, clairaudient, and clairsentient. My belief system was shaken to its core. I did not understand what was happening to me and feared I might be having a psychotic break. Although I did not know it at the time, I had experienced a soul-exchange walk-in.

You can find the full story in *Walk-Ins: Cosmology of the Soul,* but this overview gives you an idea about the confusion and magnitude of the changes that occurred.

. . . .

I often find myself reflecting on the profound shifts that have taken place since my arrival on this planet, many years ago. When I first entered onto this earthly realm, the vibrational frequency was vastly different. It was an era where the fabric of reality seemed more tightly woven into the third-dimensional paradigm. Things appeared solid, tangible, and bound by the limitations of linear time and space.

However, as time unfolded and the collective consciousness of humanity evolved, I witnessed a remarkable transformation taking place. Today, the landscape of consciousness has expanded beyond the confines of the third dimension, reaching into the realms of the fourth dimension and beyond. This shift has opened the door to a myriad of soul experiences that were unimaginable within the constraints of a strictly 3D reality.

While our physical bodies still navigate the tangible world of three-dimensional existence, our consciousness has transcended these limitations, reaching dimensions much higher and more expansive. This elevation of consciousness is the catalyst for the soul experiences that permeate our existence, allowing for a deeper understanding and exploration of our spiritual essence.

Central to this evolution are pre-birth contracts, an integral aspect of the soul's journey. Before embarking on our earthly sojourn, we engage in agreements and contracts at a soul level charting the course of our experiences and growth. These contracts serve as guiding lights leading us toward encounters and experiences that are essential for our soul's evolution.

It is through the combination of heightened consciousness and pre-birth contracts that these soul experiences become possible: soul infusions, jumper experiences, upgrades, and multidimensional incorporations, to name a few. These are all manifestations of the intricate dance between our higher consciousness and the predestined paths laid out in our pre-birth contracts.

As I reflect upon my own experiences and the transformations that have unfolded, I am reminded of the interconnectedness of all things. We are not merely passive observers in this cosmic symphony, but active participants, co-creators of our own destinies. Through the expansion of our consciousness into higher dimensions, we unlock the doorways to limitless possibilities, embracing the full spectrum of our soul's potential.

The evolution of consciousness and the fulfillment of pre-birth contracts have paved the way for the richness of soul experiences that adorn our earthly existence. As we continue to travel through the realms of time and space, may we remain ever mindful of the sacred dance between the physical and the spiritual, embracing each soul experience as a precious gift on the path toward enlightenment and self-realization.

SOUL WALK-IN EXPERIENCES

From my previous book, *Walk-Ins: Cosmology of the Soul*: "The soul—a persistent, conscious essence—will take one form after another to fulfill a given purpose each time and, thus, contribute to a collective evolution of the conscious, spiritual essence of existence itself."

Each incarnation serves as a vehicle for soul growth and enlightenment. However, I have come to realize since then that the scope of soul experiences extends far beyond what I initially conceived.

In the weaving of spiritual exploration and personal growth, individuals often find themselves immersed in a realm where conventional definitions no longer suffice. While many associate the concept of walk-ins with the arrival of a new soul, permanently exchanging places with the host body, the landscape of spiritual awakening reveals a broader spectrum of experiences that go beyond the conventional definition.

In this era, many people consider themselves to be walk-ins. However, it's crucial to discern the true essence of this phenomenon. A walk-in, in its strictest sense, denotes the permanent exchange of two souls within a single body. The popular misconception arises from the conflation of various other soul experiences that have become more prevalent due to our accelerated personal soul growth. These experiences are just as intense as a soul-exchange walk-in, and they deserve their own category. For clarity's sake, we can call these events *soul walk-in experiences*. A walk-in is one type of soul experience.

The soul's journey unfolds in myriad ways and individuals might undergo profound transformations without necessarily embodying the walk-in experience. The multifaceted nature of these experiences includes, but is not limited to step-ins, soul infusions, jumper experiences, and soul growth beyond conventional understanding. The notion of soul-exchange walk-ins can be considered just one facet of a much grander spiritual metamorphosis of soul experiences. Please keep in mind that any of the experiences discussed below can manifest through either a walk-in phenomenon or through personal spiritual practices that elevate one's physical vibration, enabling them to embody higher aspects of consciousness. In some cases, individuals embody more than one type.

TYPES OF WALK-IN EXPERIENCES

Having covered the soul-exchange walk-in soul process previously, we'll now delve into other varieties of walk-in experiences. Please keep in mind that when a new aspect enters the body, the natal soul might remain for a brief or extended observation period and then either merge, if it is from the same primary oversoul, or leave if it originates from a different primary oversoul. It will eventually depart as the new, higher frequencies render it incompatible and make it impossible to remain. If the soul originates from a different primary oversoul, it might still belong to the same soul family or soul group.

Soul Infusions: These involve the integration of higher self and oversoul aspects into the individual's soul consciousness. This infusion is not a complete exchange but rather an augmentation of the existing soul with elevated energies and wisdom. This can happen without the natal soul ever leaving the body, or if it did, a portion of the natal soul remained to be infused. It's a symbiotic process that allows the individual to access a broader spectrum of consciousness, bringing forth a heightened awareness of self and the universe.

Soul Mergers: Soul mergers resemble soul infusions, yet they differ in a significant aspect: the natal soul remains firmly intact throughout the process. During a soul merge, the complete aspect of an oversoul, sheantiaskaan, multidimensional aspects, or higher self, fuse with the natal soul. This fusion leads to a deep unification of consciousness, fostering a deeper connection and alignment with the higher aspects of the self. One or more of the higher aspects might come in. Many people believe this to be a collective experience because they have access to the fullness of the merged soul(s) experiences.

In some soul mergers, once all aspects have merged, the natal soul may leave due to the incompatible nature of the new soul aspects.

Soul Jumpers, Pop-Ins or Poppers: These refer to souls that inhabit a body for brief periods spanning from a few hours to several months. There is a brief interchange between souls where energies intertwine for a moment before returning to their respective realms. These fleeting encounters serve as catalysts for accelerated growth and expanded perspectives by providing glimpses into the vast interconnectedness of the spiritual realm.

Often, these souls have contractual agreements with the natal soul to aid during times of need, to initiate new projects, or simply to undergo the human experience. Such encounters can be extremely intense as the temporary soul begins to imprint or download its energy and alter the vibration of the host. Upon the departure, the downloads unfold leaving the host with a lingering sense of loss and a yearning for the return of the experience.

Soul Overlays: Soul overlays can take shape in either permanent or temporary forms. In this intriguing phenomenon, the natal soul remains present while another soul enters the body simultaneously, establishing a harmonious coexistence. Throughout the overlay, the natal soul assumes the role of an observer, often unaware of the unfolding events. The overlay soul envelops the natal soul, akin to a neoprene suit covering the physical body.

During this period, the overlay soul takes control while the natal soul resets, recuperates, or regroups. At times, the overlay soul may collaborate with the natal soul to fulfill a specific mission or purpose. Following the completion of this mission, either the natal soul or overlay soul may depart, or they might merge, allowing the body to be solely inhabited by the new, higher-vibrating soul. It is imperative to emphasize that this phenomenon is not a form of possession. Rather, it represents a mutually agreed upon arrangement between the souls involved.

Soul Step-Downs or Step-Ins: These experiences unveil a captivating facet within the brilliance of the soul's existence. Unlike conventional soul exchanges, where a soul permanently occupies a body, soul step-downs entail a temporary swapping of souls, each with its distinct purpose and mission. This is akin to a celestial choreographer orchestrating a Divine dance, allowing different souls to take center stage in the theater of life for a finite duration. These transient occupants arrive at the threshold of earthly existence carrying the essence of their unique purpose, poised to intertwine with the ongoing narrative of another life.

The duration of these exchanges may vary, lasting from fleeting moments to years. Yet, irrespective of the temporal span, there exists a sacred agreement, a cosmic contract that delineates the terms of engagement. Eventually, these souls will revert to their original roles, seamlessly returning to the grand production of existence. In the interim, they impart lessons, insights, and transformations that enrich both the host and the visiting soul in a symbiotic exchange of energies and experiences.

Soul Projections: This term refers to the process whereby an off-planet or extraterrestrial being projects the entirety of their soul into a human form. During this phenomenon, the original host may remain awake and aware, or they might enter a type of suspended state. This allows for the seamless integration of the projected soul into the human vessel, enabling the off-planet individual to interact and experience life on Earth directly. Some of these beings project and then enter, while others continue their existences in two places at once. Still others incarnate during the birth process. Many call this becoming a fully embodied starseed.

Soul Braids: These present a scenario where one or more souls concurrently inhabit the body, each being consciously aware of the other's presence. These souls may be positioned side-by-side or intertwined within the same energetic space. Unlike other phenomena, braided souls possess the autonomy to come and go as they please. Rather than replacing the natal soul, they attach themselves to either the natal soul or the space it occupies.

Braids often arrive to aid the natal soul in progressing to their next level of service. They collaborate with the natal soul, working in tandem to achieve shared objectives. Some braids may choose to remain for varying periods, ranging from days to an entire lifetime. Nevertheless, regardless of the duration of their stay, they always retain their individuality. When these souls eventually depart, they do so having contributed to the enrichment and growth of the natal soul. Depending on an individual's frequency, they may have the capacity to host more than one braid.

Soul Layering: This occurs when multiple aspects of the natal soul's oversoul enter a single body or energy field at birth. The oversoul is a higher-dimensional or collective consciousness that oversees the experiences, evolution, and interconnectedness of individual souls, sheantiaskaan, higher selves, or multidimensional selves. These aspects can originate from any time, place, or dimension.

Once activated, these other soul aspects intermittently enter and exit the host body for differing durations. Throughout this process, the natal soul remains intact and engages in a shared dance of experience with the activated aspects. It is not uncommon for these aspects to remain activated for extended periods, with the natal soul eventually resuming prominence. This dynamic interplay represents a co-creative dance of consciousness and experience.

SOUL TYPES

We have discussed the basic process of how a soul incarnates and acknowledges itself as an individuated Divine spark of Source—but where did we go after our individuation? Did we descend directly to Earth, traverse to a different dimension or realm of existence, or venture to another planet or star system before incarnating on planet Earth? For most, the definitive answers to these questions remain elusive. This information is accessible only to those who recollect or receive revelations through visions, meditation, or spiritual guidance.

Upon incarnation, many souls are veiled by forgetfulness, obscuring memories of past lives or the past origin of their soul. Consider the burden if we were to recollect every event from every lifetime—every war, loss, and love. Some individuals, however, retain memories of their origins and prior lives, often speaking to the emotional impact of these recollections.

There are also the fragmented souls that incarnate to call back to themselves all the aspects of their soul in a single lifetime. Fragmented souls are souls that have experienced fragmentation or division, often because of trauma, spiritual crisis, or existential challenges. These fragmented aspects of the soul may exist across different dimensions, lifetimes, or states of consciousness and may undergo a process of integration and healing to reunify and restore wholeness. I know a woman who called back all thirty-two aspects of her soul in this lifetime.

Additionally, there are collective souls, which represent a fascinating phenomenon where multiple individual souls merge together to form a unified entity or consciousness. These collective souls are formed when numerous individual souls come together, often from their higher oversoul. They are driven by shared purposes, experiences, or connections. As these individual souls merge, they contribute their unique energies, consciousness, and perspectives to create a collective consciousness that transcends the boundaries of individual identity.

Collective souls can manifest in various forms such as group consciousness, shared spiritual entities, or interconnected networks of souls. They often exhibit characteristics of synergy, collaboration, and mutual support among the individual souls that comprise them. In some belief systems, collective souls are perceived as repositories of wisdom, love, and collective evolution. They can serve as conduits for spiritual growth and transformation on a broader scale.

The concept of collective souls highlights the interconnected nature of spiritual existence and emphasizes the idea that individual souls are not isolated entities but aspects of a larger, unified whole. Exploring the dynamics of collective souls offers spiritual insights into the nature of consciousness, unity, and the interconnectedness of all beings.

Just as Gaia, often referred to as Mother Earth, embodies an upper-end seventh-density collective soul that encompasses diverse races within humanity, the universe also features a multitude of races and manifestations of soul energy.

Below are a few examples of the diverse types of souls that I have been made aware of. Each type offers unique insights into the nature, origins, and purpose of consciousness within the broader context of existence and spirituality.

Earth Seeds: These souls, native to Earth, have traveled with Gaia through each incarnation cycle, evolving through various states of being and contributing new strands of DNA throughout millennia.

Fey Souls: Fey souls originate from the realm of the *Faerie*, a mystical and enchanting dimension often depicted in folklore, mythology, and fantasy literature. In various cultural traditions, the fey—also known as faeries, fairies, or the fae—are supernatural beings associated with nature, magic, and the ethereal realms beyond human perception.

Dragon Souls: Transcending time and space, these souls incarnate from different realms or dimensions for their own spiritual growth, service, and evolution.

Source Souls or Source Seeds: Source souls, also known as Divine or primordial souls, originate directly from Prime Source, Creator, God. These souls are pure manifestations of Divine consciousness and universal love. They serve as conduits for Divine inspiration, healing, and transformation, radiating their light and essence throughout the cosmos. These pure, high-conscious souls who have never been incarnated arrive on Earth or other planets to infuse them with unconditional love, facilitating transformation and serving humanity.

Dimensional Seeds: Encompassing intradimensional, extradimensional, and multidimensional souls, these beings hail from various dimensions and may reside between dimensions.

Reincarnation or Past-Life Souls: This type of soul is incarnating from the reincarnation process of the Earth matrix where souls undergo a cyclical process of birth, death, and rebirth. Through successive incarnations, souls accumulate a wealth of diverse experiences, inhabiting different bodies, cultures, and time periods. These past lives shape the soul's journey and contribute to its ongoing evolution and spiritual growth.

Interdimensional Souls: Interdimensional souls are thought to originate from dimensions or realities beyond the physical realm, existing in parallel or alternate realities. These souls may possess multidimensional awareness, allowing them to perceive and interact with realities beyond the conventional human experience. These souls incarnate on Earth to bridge different dimensions, anchor higher frequencies of consciousness, or facilitate the integration of cosmic energies into the earthly plane.

Ascended Souls: These are souls who have undergone spiritual evolution and enlightenment, transcended the cycle of reincarnation, and achieved a higher state of consciousness. They are believed to have attained liberation, enlightenment, or ascension, transcending the limitations of earthly existence. Ascended souls may serve as guides, teachers, or spiritual mentors for those still on the path of spiritual growth and awakening. They may continue to support and inspire others from higher dimensions or realms of existence.

Elemental Souls: Believed to originate from the primordial elements that make up the fabric of the universe—such as earth, water, fire, air, and ether—these souls are thought to embody the essences and qualities of these elements. Elemental souls are associated with nature spirits, elemental beings, or mythological creatures representing the forces of nature. They work in harmony with the elements to facilitate healing, transformation, and balance in the natural world.

Angelic Souls: Angelic souls originate from the angelic realms or dimensions beyond the physical universe. These souls possess angelic qualities such as compassion, guidance, and Divine protection. Angelic souls incarnate on Earth or other realms to fulfill specific missions, offer spiritual assistance, or support the awakening of humanity.

Ancestral Souls: Believed to trace their origins back to the lineage and collective consciousness of ancestral beings and familial connections, ancestral souls carry the wisdom, traditions, and genetic imprints of their ancestors. They also inherit blessings, karma, and ancestral wounds, which can influence their relationships and the path of their spiritual journey.

Starseeds: These are souls originating from different planets, galaxies, star systems, or realms, who incarnate on Earth to serve humanity and elevate consciousness. Often spiritually evolved, they may feel disconnected from Earth and possess a mission of spiritual service.

Indigo, Crystal, and Rainbow Souls: Hailing from diverse parts of the galaxy, these souls assist humanity in the ascension process, often exhibiting supernatural gifts and awakening fully aware of their origins and abilities.

Wanderer Souls: Lowering their vibrational frequency to inhabit human bodies, these souls traverse time, space, and dimensions to raise consciousness and gather information. They often struggle with feelings of isolation and may exhibit physical ailments.

Hybrid Souls: Combinations of souls from various systems, galaxies or realms, these ascended beings return to Earth for specialized functions, bringing transformation and order to chaos.

Multidimensional Souls: These occur when aspects of the soul from other spaces and times merge with the individual's soul. This merging facilitates a continuous flow of information and expands the individual's awareness beyond their current time and space.

Many individuals are currently undergoing intense soul experiences through upgrades, a process where their energetic systems are refined and aligned with higher frequencies. This involves anchoring additional frequency of their higher selves and oversouls, which unlocks dormant potentials and capacities. These upgrades are like cosmic software updates, enhancing the individual's abilities and understanding of their soul's purpose. Upgrades may or may not involve a walk-in experience.

Incorporating multidimensional aspects is yet another dimension of soul evolution. This entails the integration of facets from parallel realities and dimensions, enriching the individual with diverse experiences and perspectives. These multidimensional aspects contribute to the soul's expansion and facilitate a deeper understanding of the interconnected web of existence.

People might be undergoing these transformative experiences without consciously recognizing them. The veil between the physical and spiritual realms is thinning, allowing for a deeper integration of spiritual energies into everyday life. Instead of labeling these experiences solely as walk-ins, it is imperative to acknowledge the diverse and nuanced ways in which souls are evolving and expanding their consciousness.

The era we find ourselves in is witnessing an unprecedented surge in spiritual awakening and personal growth. The conventional definition of walk-ins, while valid for some, does not encapsulate the breadth and depth of soul experiences occurring on this planet. As individuals undergo soul infusions, jumper experiences, upgrades, and multidimensional incorporations, the true essence of their spiritual journey unveils itself as transcending the limitations of language and conventional understanding. By understanding these soul experiences, we can embrace the vast and intricate nature of our spiritual evolution, recognizing that each path is as unique as the soul that embarks upon it.

COSMIC CONVERGENCE

We now find ourselves standing at the crossroads of a cosmic convergence, where the threads of individual destinies are intertwined with the vast tapestry of the universe. From understanding the diverse types of walk-ins to unraveling the mysteries of the incarnation process and exploring the varied origins of souls, our journey has been one of revelation and enlightenment.

In delving into the different types of walk-ins, we have witnessed a kaleidoscope of experiences, from soul exchanges to infusions, overlays, braids, and more. Each narrative has offered a unique lens through which to perceive the multifaceted nature of these cosmic travelers. As we embrace the diversity of walk-in experiences, we find a collective story that transcends the limitations of individuality and speaks to the interconnectedness of all souls.

The exploration of the incarnation process has unveiled the intricate dance between the ethereal and the earthly. It is a process where souls from various corners of the cosmos choose to don the earthly garment and embark on a voyage of self-discovery, growth, and service. This cosmic dance, orchestrated by the unseen hands of destiny, echoes through the corridors of time, shaping the evolution of both the individual and the collective soul.

Turning our gaze to the origins of souls, we've ventured beyond the veil of forgetfulness to glimpse the vastness from which souls emerge. Each category tells a story of cosmic heritage and purpose. The recognition that souls come from diverse solar systems, galaxies, and dimensions invites us to expand our understanding of existence beyond the confines of earthly boundaries. Yet, these views are only the tip of the iceberg. The vastness of the cosmos and the convergence of the souls' plasmatic incarnational experience into form continue to reveal many mysteries.

In our exploration of the soul from its inception at birth to the phenomenon of walk-ins, we are reminded that this experience is not merely an intellectual exercise; it involves immersion into the essence of our cosmic being. It is an acknowledgment that our soul's journey transcends the boundaries of a single lifetime, weaving our individual stories into the grand tapestry of existence.

May this information serve as an invitation to delve deeper into the mysteries that surround us, to question the limits of our understanding, and to embrace the vastness of the cosmic dance in which we all participate.

In the following section, Barbara Lamb shares what hypnotic regression is and regressions featuring individuals who identify themselves as walk-ins.

HYPNOTIC REGRESSION THERAPY

Regression therapy is an excellent method of finding out about important experiences that people have had earlier in life or in previous lifetimes. It can uncover the meaning and purpose of someone's conditions, traits, or reactions. This kind of therapy involves using the process of hypnosis—a deep state of relaxation. Hypnosis can guide us to the source of our physical symptoms or emotional reactions to certain things, people, and places. It might reveal unusual experiences we have had, including anomalous or paranormal events.

In my psychotherapy practice, which began in 1976, and in my regression therapy work, which began in 1984, I have conducted hypnotic regressions on several thousand people. These regressions have taken us to a multitude of lifetimes and experiences. Some of the experiences clients have described are relatively unknown—yet they have happened. Some have occurred on Earth, and others happened off-planet in various spacecrafts, on different planets, or in different dimensions.

Regressions have answered thousands of questions for my clients, including some they wondered about for decades. This kind of therapy can bring into conscious awareness the details of anomalous experiences that people have had during a non-conscious state of being. It is evident that the subconscious parts of our minds record every detail of what we experience, including those things we were not consciously aware of at the time. Through regression, we can learn about important events that have affected us greatly, which can help our lives make more sense.

An important aspect of this work is that the soul of the person being regressed is always involved in the process. The soul contains the memories of every moment of every incarnation and every state of being that we have experienced. In regressions, we tap into the soul, the higher self, and the spirit guides, asking them to assist in the process of discovery and finding meaning. This often results in the person recognizing their true purpose for coming into this life. Once they identify their true purpose, which they chose at the soul level before incarnating in this lifetime, they are usually motivated to carry out that purpose.

I first became aware of the phenomenon of walk-ins in 1991 when, at a past-life therapy conference, I talked with some of my colleagues over breakfast. One therapist told us of a client she had worked with for several sessions, trying to get to the source of her severe allergies to almost everything on Earth. The regression showed that this client had been an extraterrestrial being earlier in this life and had been perfectly adapted to that kind of body, digestive system, food, and environment. She wanted to (and was guided to) come to Earth to help humanity. Instead of waiting for the opportunity to be conceived, gestated, and born on Earth and then spending years growing to adulthood, she chose a more expedient way. She looked from afar at many people on Earth and found a woman who did not really want to be here in life anymore. Although this woman wasn't consciously aware of it, her soul was contacted by the soul of the extraterrestrial female, and they made an agreement: the woman on Earth would leave the body at an appointed time and place, and her soul would return to the spirit realm. The extraterrestrial being would inhabit the woman's body for the rest of her Earth life. They mutually agreed to make this soul exchange.

The walk-in found it difficult to be here eating our kind of food, breathing our kind of air, and dealing with our pollution, viruses, bacteria, density, emotions, etc. The woman's body she inhabited reacted badly to all these stressors. She needed hypnosis assistance to acclimate better to these aspects of being on Earth so she could carry out the mission for which she had come.

I was truly impressed by the knowledge that extremely different types of beings could arrive here and live a life on Earth as a human so they could assist humanity. I began keeping a lookout for other possible walk-ins.

WALK-IN HYPNOTIC REGRESSION SESSION #1

A women came to me for regression work in the mid-1990s, saying that she no longer felt like herself. She had lost interest in her successful career in the finance industry and felt strongly attracted to learning how to do hypnosis and to help people with this method. Her partner noticed these changes and was concerned about her lack of enthusiasm in her work. Tensions were arising between them. The woman had ceased doing the household chores she had previously done and was no longer contributing income to the upkeep of their home. To her partner, she seemed to have become a stranger who had her head in the clouds. The partner was especially concerned with her wish to learn hypnosis and use only that skill for income.

During her first regression, she relived the unusual experience of a soul exchange. She remembered willingly leaving her body and allowing another soul to inhabit it. This happened in the middle of the night. The woman's partner noticed her moving strangely and murmuring unusual sounds while asleep but had no idea of what was happening. At some point, the woman said goodbye—yet her body remained there.

During the regression, we also heard from the point of view of the incoming soul. That soul had been living as a different kind of being out in space. It knew it was taking on a huge challenge by agreeing to live in a woman's body on Earth. It knew it would have to make numerous adaptations to live a human life. This soul was leaving a life of being a commander of a spaceship, was male in gender, and what we call an extraterrestrial being. From his point of view, it was apparent that humans residing on Earth needed help in overcoming their negative habits, emotions, addictions, conflicts, aggressiveness, greed, narcissism, etc. to survive as a species. His distant ancestors had helped to create humans, and he and his fellow beings had maintained a strong interest in helping them.

He chose this woman for the soul exchange because she didn't want to be in her life anymore and was willing to leave; because she had effective business skills and a desire to help people with hypnosis; and because she already had a supportive partner to share life with. That partner could show him how to function in the Earth's culture. He saw this as an appropriate opportunity for helping humans without going through the long process of dying from his current extraterrestrial form and reincarnating as a human being. It was much more expedient to come into a life on Earth and do the work he was deeply moved to do.

This walk-in woman and her partner joined my Experiencer Support Group and learned about the existence of otherworldly beings who visited people for many purposes. Neither of them had known about this reality before having that regression and subsequently hearing from the other group participants. The group helped them to accept and understand the mysterious changes that had happened to my client.

A subsequent regression with me revealed an additional aspect of her experiences. Through brief conscious memories and through the regression process, she realized that every few weeks, she would leave her bed in the middle of the night, return to the ship, and become her male extraterrestrial counterpart: the commander aspect of herself flying the ship. She was always welcomed back on the ship and was respected for her leadership, her flying skill, and her courage in changing her gender and living and functioning on Earth. These episodes of visiting the ship and resuming his piloting duties were both rewarding and exciting.

As time went on, having adjusted reasonably to human life and to being a different gender, my client was trained in hypnotherapy and created a career of helping people with many kinds of problems. The personal partnership, which was already strained, became more so and eventually ended in dissolution—but the mission of the walk-in continued.

WALK-IN HYPNOTIC REGRESSION SESSION #2

In the late 1990s, a friend took me to meet a woman she considered exceptionally spiritually oriented and other worldly. We met at this woman's home one afternoon and I was surprised to find her dressed in a long, flowing white gown and wearing a tiara of fresh flowers in her hair with a Christian cross hanging from her neck. She appeared to be in her thirties, and she was quite lovely in a natural way. Instead of doing the usual introductory chit-chat, this woman began talking about the Christ and other spiritual matters. She was well-versed in the New Testament and other spiritual writings. She made it known that she considered her mission to be raising people's consciousness to a more spiritual level and said she was eager to begin this work. She said she had been here for only a few months. It turned out that she had been here in this life for only that short period of time.

That entire afternoon and early evening, we talked about her desire to stimulate people's spirituality and growth. She saw most people as having a three-dimensional, superficial, materialistic point of view, but knew they were limited by their lack of awareness and having no sense of purpose in life. This was causing problems on Earth, she said. She was determined to change that and make a significant contribution to humanity.

During a hypnotic regression, we focused on going to the source of her determination to awaken spiritual awareness in people. We learned she had come from a higher dimension of reality, a spiritual realm where she was not living in a physical body. This was a beautiful, celestial realm full of light and love and the awareness of God, the Source. All beings in that realm functioned wonderfully well together, without conflicts, wars, or difficulties. From that realm and frequency, she had awareness of the physical, third-dimensional planet Earth and the many difficulties and conflicts the inhabitants were having there. She thought these physical inhabitants on Earth should know of the more wonderful ways of being and living, as experienced in the higher-frequency celestial realms. She decided to show them ways to raise their frequencies and consciousness, so they could have a more peaceful, loving existence while accepting each other's differences.

To accomplish that goal, she would have to live here on Earth among us. She found a woman who was dissatisfied with life and did not want to continue to live anymore. That woman had an active life with a like-minded husband. They were members of a motorcycle club for couples, and, on most weekends, they toured around with their club members, making lots of noise and raising a lot of dust wherever they went. They enjoyed camping as well as drinking and smoking various substances. They were a rough and ready group without a spiritual thought in their minds. The walk-out woman (the natal) had adapted to participate in this way of life.

After this higher-dimensional being did the soul exchange, trouble began to develop in the marriage. The husband wanted to continue their rowdy way of life and was shocked that she was no longer interested in motorcycle tours and camping trips. Instead of wearing jeans and boots, she began to wear lovely dresses. She became gentler and more gracious. She gave up eating meat, drinking alcohol, smoking cigarettes, and using drugs. His confusion led to anger.

Even though she had been here for only a few months, it was apparent that they would not be continuing their marriage. They divorced and she went on to do the work she had come to Earth to do.

WALK-IN HYPNOTIC REGRESSION SESSION #3

A man in France approached me for an online regression in 2021 because he didn't understand why he felt so different from everyone he knew. He had wondered about this for many years. He said he did not remember much about his early childhood except that his family and other people somehow seemed like strangers. He did not feel his family were his *real* family, even though they insisted they were. He felt nervous and shy and did not enjoy playing with other children. He avoided most people because he felt so different from them.

Beginning at approximately age six, he frequently went into the nearby forest by himself, where he saw beings who were distinctly different from all the humans he knew. Among them was a tall man with golden skin and yellow-white hair who wore a long robe. The man was accompanied by a lovely adult female. They both floated in the air. The man also saw elf-like people who had long hair, long ears, large eyes, and shiny golden skin. They dressed in peculiar clothes and moved slowly. He felt that these beings were his protectors, so he enjoyed being with them and felt safe in their presence.

As an adult, a medical scan revealed many small, implanted objects in his body. Neither he nor his doctor understood what these objects were or where they had come from, but they suspected something unusual had been happening to him. In a subsequent past-life regression, he learned he had been a space traveler in a previous life. This was something he had a nice feeling about, as if it were somehow familiar to him.

We chose the focus for the regression to be the source of his feeling like an outsider. He found himself in another realm with the safe, loving beings who he had often seen in the forest when he was a boy. They did not have dense, physical bodies. They seemed more ethereal, almost transparent, and they floated. He became aware that he was one of them, living in that non-physical world in a loving, caring life. He learned that he had been aware of Earth, its human population, and he was aware that they needed to learn to be more loving and accepting of people who had different skin colors or were from different cultures. He could see the misery this non-acceptance was causing for those who were different. He had a strong urge to go to Earth and help the people to be more loving and accepting of each other, as his people were. His fellow beings gave him encouragement to do this. They promised to visit him on Earth and assist him in his mission.

He had chosen to enter into a soul exchange with a six-year-old Black boy who lived in a Caucasian culture in France. This boy had severe physical difficulties and was unhappy with his life. His family and his doctor thought he did not have much time to live and that he was ready to leave. The soul of the man met with the soul of the boy, they made their agreement, and they did the soul exchange when the boy was passing on. No one else knew this was happening. They only knew the boy had survived.

Once my client was residing in the boy's human body, it was different than he had expected. He was blocked from knowing who he was, where he had come from, and why he was suddenly here. No one knew the exchange had happened and probably wouldn't have understood it or believed it if they had known. So, he continued growing up as that boy, feeling sad and lonely and different.

In the regression, he realized he had chosen to do a soul exchange with that particular child because he would have a richness of experience as well as the continual challenge of trying to get along with people of different races and cultures. This would inspire him to help people be more accepting and loving. He wanted to help humanity be more tolerant of each other, no matter what their differences were. He knew this lifetime would give him the training for waking people up and for doing the work he came to do.

Living in a body was often painful for him. He knew he was supposed to be a human, but he still had a sense of the type of being he had been and who he sensed he really was. He was not really human—and yet, he was here living as a human and having people assume he was a human.

His other-worldly advisors told him: "You are not from here (Earth). You came here to live among people and to lift them up to better ways. You know so many things and give so much, but we block your memories of your identity so you won't show people who you really are, as you might be in danger from their reactions. Your body is not your real body. You feel like a failure. You feel empty. But you can get back to feeling your true self and expressing yourself, and you'll feel good. You don't understand people and what they care about and talk about and are interested in. You don't feel human. It's understandable."

He felt safe and supported with these beings, who continued to visit him in the forest, even in his adult life. They appeared as lights and power rather than as beings with distinct faces. They seemed to be from somewhere else and yet they felt like family.

This client learned from the regression that his difficult experiences growing up were just experiences to learn from. He realized he would eventually understand who he really was by reconnecting with his fellow beings. He knew that would include being connected to all life everywhere and to the oneness, the true Source.

I invited him to let himself experience being his original, true self and fully indulge in it. He allowed himself to remember and feel that, and it was a glorious experience. He realized he could be a great help to humans by being who he really is, full of acceptance, love, and oneness. People would pick up on these feelings from him and be enhanced by them and pass them along to others.

He was grateful for his regression session and became more dedicated than ever to completing his mission here on Earth. He now understands his walk-in experience and what he is here to do.

WALK-IN HYPNOTIC REGRESSION SESSION #4

A woman came to me for a regression, saying a psychic had told her she might be a walk-in from another star system. She did not know what a walk-in was, or anything about other star systems. She came to find out about her true life's mission and why she felt so different from all the other people in her life. She worked as a nurse at a hospital doing standard American Medical Association work and was involved in scientific research. She was considering quitting her work in endocrinology because she was drawn to doing direct healing. Before she quit her job, she wanted to know what her true purpose was in life.

In the regression, we asked for guidance from her higher self—her soul—about her real purpose for being here. She found herself in another realm rather than on Earth. She was a different kind of being: a seven-foot-tall female with long, blond-white hair, bright blue eyes, and pale white skin. She wore a long robe and was with several beings of the same kind. They had heard about human beings who lived on a planet called Earth. She was happy doing healing work with these lovely companions. They were gentle, loving kin and were tuned in to Source. The work was fun. Their patients were the same kind of beings. The healing room was metal and glass and filled with light. It was a happy existence for her. She did her healing with a glowing sphere of light between her hands, which she slowly moved over the whole body of the one who needed healing. This sphere was energy and could heal any defects or conditions in the body.

Unfortunately, she was captured and taken by some other, negative beings to a different spaceship full of unlikeable beings who had scaly skin and different facial features. They had learned about her and her amazing healing abilities and wanted her to heal them. There were beings of many types coming to their ship for healing and leaving when they were healed. She heartedly disliked being there. She had been forced to go there, and she felt like a slave, controlled by these negative, reptile-like beings. She longed to go back to her original planet to be with her own kind.

Eventually a male of a different species came to the spaceship for healing and recognized her unhappiness. He managed to remove her from that ship and prepared her for going to planet Earth. It would involve her making a soul exchange with a human who was getting ready to leave her body. He brought her into contact with a four-year-old girl who was nearing the end of her life due to major physical malfunctions. The soul of my client and the soul of the little girl made a contract for the girl to leave her body and return to the spiritual realm from which she had come, so that my client's soul could enter her body and live a relatively long life as a human being and as a healer of other humans.

Because the parents of that little girl were scientifically oriented, they made sure that the girl (my client) would have a scientific education. Even though the girl spoke of wishing to do natural healing, the parents insisted that she train as a nurse in the standard medical field. She was successful in that field, but she continued to feel she should be helping people with different methods.

After her regression, she realized she needed to bring love, happiness, and positivity into her healing work. She left her nursing job and took some courses in natural healing with energy from her hands. She is now doing that work effectively and has also developed remote healing. She is fulfilling her soul's purpose for her life.

The woman recently had some experiences that validated her having come to Earth from somewhere else. She remembers looking in a mirror when she was a little girl and being shocked by not recognizing herself. Her brother reminded her that, as a girl, she often spoke a strange language in her sleep. In her childhood, she also had a vivid dream of looking at a screen which zoomed in from high above on a house on Earth with a masculine voice behind her saying she would live there with that family in that house. She had never flown in an airplane or seen an aerial view before having that dream.

WALK-IN HYPNOTIC REGRESSION SESSION #5

This case study is about a woman who already knew that she was a walk-in but was seeking clarity and validation of her mission here on Earth. In the regression, she relived the experience of living with her fellow beings on the other side. She called them her collective and talked about how they arrived on the Earth plane and why she was selected to represent the collective aspect on Earth.

She described herself and her collective this way: "We are like a wave of energy, flowing and moving as one. We are vibration, light, sound, and frequency. We have awareness, consciousness, and intellect. We do not have a physical body or a location. We don't have names for ourselves, as we are frequency and we communicate telepathically. We are connected souls, although we have some individuality. Most of the time, we think of ourselves as one—unless an aspect of us pulls away to go to another planet or star system to have a completely different type of experience. We also contain the consciousness of other souls who want to go to a physical place: a planet called Earth. It feels like there is a request for help from Earth, from the many beings who live there, and it's pulling us.

"I've never been there before, and I want to be part of the energy of spiritually waking up. The collective's experiences are not like those on Earth, but we do feel compassion for humans and for the Earth itself. I'll go and help wake up the consciousness of the beings on that planet.

"To do that, I must live on the planet in a human form. I understand that a body has been chosen for me to live in and an agreement has been made. It is a physical structure with many problems, and the soul wants to be released from it. We can hear the cry of that soul to be released. It was decided that I, this aspect of the collective, would trade places with that person on Earth. The agreement was made in a split second.

"Vibration and prayers are coming to us. We are hearing and feeling it and we are agreeing. The soul I am trading places with has already gotten everything she needed to learn in this lifetime. She was unhappy. She is dying and leaving her life.

"It is important for me to know she is very ill and is inspiring me to come to her. She is closed-minded, so if I can open her mind and body to who she really is, others can do the same with other humans. She is a good example of not knowing and being limited and unaware. I'll go to Earth and wake up her and others by living in her body. Once I am in her body, I will remain there, if her body lives. We are sparkles of light, twinkles of light, pure thought, with a group consciousness, full of knowledge and awareness. We are what many humans on Earth want to become.

"During the soul exchange, the natal soul is taken to an Arcturian ship while I'm going into the woman's body through the top of her head. The woman is leaving through her chest, all at the same moment. Her soul is going to an Arcturian ship, and she is given a new body. She can no longer function in her old body, although she is less than forty years old. Arcturus is where she had come from before her Earth life, although she didn't know that and wouldn't have believed it.

"I am in her body now and I can't breathe! I'm sitting up in bed and my eyes are opening. I'm thinking I am somewhere else with my sparkly energy forms, but I'm not! I don't know what's going on. My mind is cloudy. It's strange being in a body! This body needs to be fixed! Everything is slow here. It will take a long to heal on Earth, but quick in my time. I'm beginning to remember things that had been wired into her mind, including glimpses of past lives."

As a walk-in, this woman changed greatly. Although she was instantaneously healed, she found ways to continually restore her body. She left her husband and moved to a different state with the children they had had, and she learned from special teachers that she was a walk-in. Before she understood that, she had thought she was crazy.

It was difficult to go from being infinite and formless to being contained in a physical body. "It was a delicate process, a re-wiring," she said. The woman she exchanged with would not have believed any of that. It had been pre-arranged that she would find the right teachers. "It's like magnets pulling toward each other." By working with other teachers, they helped her to realize that she was a walk-in. Afterwards, she worked with many people to wake them up to who they truly are.

She realizes that this was her purpose. "The people are confused. They are like little ants on an ant hill. They don't know what they are doing. They are frantic. Not everyone wants to be awakened and not many people try to wake them up. We're all just energy, but most of them think they are people."

Currently, she is helping people to realize their spiritual nature through her teachings and providing a platform for people to share their spiritual insights.

"The frequency which I come from is surrounding the Earth. The soul is like a blanket. Sometimes, we come into human form and help people feel good. Because people cannot realize who they are when they are feeling pain, I heal the pain first. Then I can help them develop spiritual awareness."

A NEW REALITY

The exploration of the walk-in phenomena offers insights into the intricate nature and complexity of consciousness. The concept of walk-ins invites contemplation on the diverse types of souls and their origins. Individuals have recounted transformative experiences characterized by significant shifts in identity, personality, and life purpose often attributed to the arrival of a new soul or consciousness.

In this segment, we delved into the intriguing phenomenon of walk-ins, wherein individuals undergo a transformative experience involving the exchange or arrival of a new consciousness or soul. Through various narratives and accounts, we sought to unravel the intricacies of this phenomenon, unveiling the multifaceted nature of walk-ins and their impact on the lives of those who undergo such profound experiences.

The incarnation process of the soul was a focal point, shedding light on the diverse perspectives and beliefs surrounding how souls come into existence and enter the realm of the physical. Whether through Divine creation, cosmic origins, or as part of a collective consciousness, the ways in which souls are conceptualized contribute to spiritual understanding.

Expanding our exploration, we ventured into the realm of different types of souls, each possessing unique qualities, origins, and purposes. From individual souls, which are intricately tied to personal identity and life experiences, to collective souls formed through the merging of multiple individual essences, we navigated through the diverse manifestations of consciousness.

To recap, individual souls, which enter a person at birth (natal soul), represent the essence and identity of a single individual. Conversely, collective souls are conglomerates of multiple individual souls that merge to form a unified group consciousness, fostering interconnectedness and unity among the individual aspects.

Both types of souls are perceived to have various origins. Some are associated with the Earth itself, deeply rooted in earthly experiences and energies, while others originate from celestial realms beyond our own.

Furthermore, there are cosmic souls connected with the vast expanse of the universe and angelic souls associated with celestial beings and higher realms of existence. These diverse origins reflect the multifaceted nature of consciousness and the interconnectedness of souls within the broader framework of existence.

The exploration of walk-in phenomena through hypnotic regressions offers intriguing insights into the complexities of consciousness and the potential for soul exchange or transition between individuals. Through these regressions, participants have recounted profound transformative experiences of undergoing significant shifts in identity, personality, and life purpose often attributed to the arrival of a new soul or consciousness into their bodies.

The hypnotic regressions have revealed diverse narratives of walk-in experiences ranging from sudden awakenings to gradual transitions and encompassing a spectrum of emotions, sensations, and memories associated with the integration of a new consciousness. Participants have described feelings of disorientation, confusion, and identity crisis as well as moments of clarity, purpose, and spiritual awakening following the arrival of a walk-in soul.

Regressions have shed light on the dynamics between the departing soul and the incoming consciousness, highlighting themes of mutual agreement, soul contracts, and karmic connections between the individuals involved. Participants have expressed a sense of gratitude, acceptance, and reverence for the journey facilitated by the walk-in experience. They recognized it as a catalyst for personal growth, healing, and spiritual evolution.

While the phenomenon of walk-ins remains enigmatic and subject to varying interpretations, the hypnotic regressions provide a platform for individuals to explore and make sense of their unique experiences within a safe and supportive environment. By delving into the depths of consciousness through regression therapy, participants can gain valuable insights, clarity, and healing, ultimately empowering them to embrace and integrate the transformative potentials of their walk-in experiences into their lives.

Join us in the next section as we begin to unravel the mysteries of starseeds.

SECTION TWO
STARSEEDS

EXPLORING THE COSMIC ORIGINS OF HUMAN SOULS

In the vast expanse of the cosmos, amidst the swirling galaxies and shimmering stars, there exists a lineage of souls whose origins trace back to distant realms beyond our earthly comprehension. These souls, known as starseeds, are beings of light and wisdom who have incarnated on Earth to play a unique role in the unfolding of human evolution.

Starseeds carry within them the essence of celestial realms and cosmic wisdom, imbued with the knowledge and experience of lifetimes spent traversing the cosmos. Their journey is one of awakening and remembrance as they seek to reconnect with their true origins and fulfill their sacred purpose on this planet.

But what exactly is a starseed and what sets them apart from the rest of humanity? At their core, starseeds are souls who have originated from distant stars, galaxies, or dimensions, answering the call to incarnate on Earth during this pivotal moment in history. They are the cosmic pioneers and way-showers, here to assist humanity in its collective evolution and spiritual awakening.

Starseeds come in many forms and from various cosmic lineages, each carrying unique gifts, talents, and missions. Some may resonate with the energy of the Pleiades, Sirius, Arcturus, or other star systems, while others might embody the essence of angelic realms, elemental beings, or interdimensional travelers. Yet, regardless of their origin, all starseeds share a common purpose: to anchor the frequencies of higher consciousness and Divine love onto the Earth plane. In essence, they are extraterrestrial, dimensional souls and source seeds.

Throughout history, starseeds have played a crucial role in guiding humanity toward greater understanding, compassion, and unity. They have been the visionaries, teachers, and healers who have led by example, inspiring others to awaken to their own divinity and reclaim their cosmic heritage. And as we stand on the precipice of a new era of enlightenment, the presence of starseeds among us serves as a beacon of hope and inspiration for the future of our planet.

In spiritual and metaphysical circles, a starseed is a term used to describe individuals who originated from another planet, star system, or dimension and incarnated on Earth with a specific mission or purpose. Starseeds are thought to possess an innate sense of cosmic connection, often feeling like they don't fully belong on Earth. They might long for a sense of home that transcends earthly experiences.

The concept of starseeds suggests that these individuals carry unique energetic signatures or soul origins that distinguish them from typical Earth inhabitants. They are believed to possess advanced spiritual abilities, heightened intuition, and a deep sense of empathy and compassion for all living beings.

The origins of starseeds are diverse and varied. Some of them identify with specific star systems, planets, or galactic civilizations, including these:

Pleiadian starseeds are believed to originate from the Pleiades star cluster. They are often associated with creativity, sensitivity, and spiritual wisdom. Pleiadian starseeds are said to embody a deep connection to nature and possess advanced healing abilities.

Sirian starseeds come from the Sirius star system, particularly Sirius A and Sirius B. They are known for their leadership qualities, courage, and loyalty. Sirian starseeds are believed to have a strong connection to water and may possess advanced technological knowledge.

Lyran starseeds hail from the Lyra constellation. They are characterized by their courage, creativity, and pioneering spirit. Lyran starseeds are believed to have played a significant role in the seeding of humanoid civilizations in the Milky Way galaxy.

Andromedan starseeds come from the Andromeda galaxy. They are known for their deep understanding of universal truths and their commitment to spiritual evolution. Andromedan starseeds may possess advanced psychic abilities and a strong sense of empathy.

Orion starseeds originate from the Orion constellation. They are often associated with strength, resilience, and a deep sense of purpose. Orion starseeds are said to be adept at navigating challenges and bringing balance to chaotic situations.

Arcturian starseeds originate from the Arcturus star system. They are known for their advanced spiritual knowledge, healing abilities, and dedication to service. Arcturian starseeds are said to embody the principles of love, compassion, and unity consciousness.

Venusian starseeds come from the planet Venus. They are associated with beauty, harmony, and the arts. Venusian starseeds are believed to have a deep connection to the natural world and a profound appreciation for aesthetic beauty.

Mintakan starseeds originate from the Mintaka star system in the Orion constellation. They are known for their strong intuition, intellectual abilities, and love of learning. Mintakan starseeds may feel a deep connection to nature and a strong desire to explore the mysteries of the universe.

Urmah starseeds are believed to have originated from feline-like extraterrestrial civilizations. They are known for their grace, agility, and independence. These starseeds may possess psychic abilities, heightened intuition, and a strong sense of loyalty to their spiritual family. They are also quite warrior-like.

Maldek starseeds are associated with the ancient planet Malde, which is said to have been destroyed in a cataclysmic event. They are known for their resilience, adaptability, and ability to overcome adversity. Maldek starseeds may possess advanced healing abilities and a deep connection to the Earth.

Avian starseeds originate from bird-like extraterrestrial civilizations. They are known for their freedom-loving nature, creativity, and connection to the skies. Avian starseeds may possess psychic abilities, a strong affinity for flight, and a deep appreciation for beauty and harmony.

Martian starseeds come from the planet Mars. They are associated with qualities such as courage, determination, and innovation. Martian starseeds may possess advanced technological knowledge, leadership abilities, and a pioneering spirit.

Polarian starseeds are believed to come from the ancient civilization of Polaris, which is said to have existed in the northern polar region of Earth. They are known for their wisdom and patience, as well as their deep reverence for nature and the elements.

Lemurian starseeds are linked to the ancient civilization of Lemuria, which is said to have existed in the Pacific Ocean thousands of years ago. They are known for their deep connection to the Earth, wisdom, and spiritual teachings.

Atlantean starseeds are associated with the ancient civilization of Atlantis, which is believed to have existed in the Atlantic Ocean. They are known for their advanced technological knowledge, psychic abilities, and spiritual wisdom.

Indigo children are believed to possess innate spiritual gifts and a strong sense of purpose. They are often characterized by their rebellious nature, sensitivity, and intuitive abilities. Indigo children are said to have come to Earth to usher in a new era of consciousness and transformation.

Crystal children are young starseeds. They arrived on Earth after the Indigo children. They are believed to possess even higher levels of spiritual awareness, empathy, and sensitivity. Crystal children are known for their gentle nature, psychic abilities, and connection to the natural world.

Rainbow children are another type of starseed and are the most spiritually advanced generation of starseeds. They are characterized by their pure hearts, unconditional love, and ability to radiate healing energy. Rainbow children are said to be here to bring harmony and unity to the world.

Lightworkers are starseeds who have incarnated on Earth with a specific mission to spread love, light, and healing energy. They are often drawn to spiritual practices, holistic healing modalities, and humanitarian causes.

Lightworkers may possess a variety of spiritual gifts and talents to assist in their mission.

Other Star Systems and Galaxies: Starseeds may also identify with other star systems, galaxies, or dimensions, each with its unique characteristics, qualities, and missions.

WAKING UP

When a starseed becomes aware of its cosmic origins and embraces its identity, this revelation often marks the beginning of a spiritual awakening and personal transformation. The following describes what typically happens to a starseed upon this realization.

The first step for a starseed is often a deep, inner knowing or sense of recognition that they are not solely human but possess a cosmic heritage. This realization may come through dreams, synchronicities, or spiritual experiences that trigger a remembrance of their identity.

As starseeds awaken to their cosmic origins, they begin to integrate higher-dimensional wisdom and knowledge into their consciousness. They may recall past-life memories, receive downloads of information from higher realms, or experience heightened intuitive abilities that allow them to access universal truths and insights.

With awareness of their starseed identity comes a profound sense of purpose and mission. Starseeds feel called to contribute to the collective awakening and evolution of humanity, often through acts of service, healing, or sharing their unique gifts and talents with the world. They may feel a deep resonance with specific causes or spiritual teachings that align with their soul's purpose.

The awakening process for a starseed is often accompanied by intense periods of inner growth and healing. They may confront unresolved traumas, limiting beliefs, or karmic patterns that are ready to be released and transmuted. This inner work allows starseeds to align more fully with their higher selves and embody their true essence.

As starseeds awaken to their cosmic identity, they often feel a deep longing to connect with others who share a similar resonance and understanding. They may seek out communities of like-minded individuals, soul family members, or spiritual mentors who can provide support, guidance, and validation.

Embracing their starseed identity empowers individuals to step into their authentic power and sovereignty. Starseeds who recognize their inherent worthiness and divinity can reclaim their innate abilities to co-create their reality and manifest their highest potential. This self-realization allows starseeds to live more fully in alignment with their soul's purpose and vision for their life.

Overall, the awakening of a starseed marks the beginning of a transformation that includes self-discovery, spiritual growth, and cosmic remembrance. This is a deeply sacred process that unfolds with grace and Divine guidance, leading starseeds to a greater understanding of their cosmic heritage and their destined role in the grand tapestry of existence.

CHARACTERISTICS

Identifying as a starseed is a deeply personal and intuitive process. There is no definitive checklist or set of criteria to determine if you are one. However, many individuals who resonate with the starseed concept often experience certain signs or characteristics that suggest a cosmic connection or origin.

Next are some common signs that you might be a starseed.

Feeling of Not Belonging: Starseeds often feel like they don't fully belong on Earth and may experience a sense of homesickness or longing for a place they can't quite identify.

Deep Spiritual Awareness: Starseeds tend to possess a strong sense of spirituality from a young age, often questioning the nature of reality and seeking deeper truths about existence.

Heightened Sensitivity: Starseeds are often highly empathic and sensitive to energy, emotions, and the environment around them. They may feel overwhelmed in crowded or chaotic environments and seek solitude to recharge.

Strong Intuition: Starseeds often have a strong inner knowing or intuition that guides them in their lives. They may receive intuitive insights, messages, or guidance from higher realms or cosmic sources.

Unusual Dreams or Memories: Starseeds may have vivid dreams or memories of otherworldly experiences, encounters with extraterrestrial beings, or lifetimes in different dimensions or star systems.

Fascination with Space and the Stars: Starseeds often have a deep fascination with space, astronomy, and extraterrestrial life. They may feel drawn to stargazing, astrology, or science fiction.

Feeling Different or Unique: Starseeds often feel like they are different from those around them. They may have unconventional interests, perspectives, or experiences that set them apart.

Strong Mission or Purpose: Starseeds often feel a strong sense that they have a purpose in life, a calling to make a positive difference in the world, or a longing to assist in humanity's spiritual evolution.

Unexplained Physical or Psychic Abilities: Starseeds may possess physical or psychic abilities such as telepathy, clairvoyance, energy healing, or channeling.

Synchronicities and Cosmic Connections: Starseeds may experience synchronicities, serendipitous events, or meaningful coincidences that seem to align with their spiritual path or cosmic mission.

Drawn to Ancient Wisdom: Starseeds often feel a strong connection to ancient civilizations, wisdom teachings, and spiritual practices from cultures around the world. They may resonate with concepts such as sacred geometry, mysticism, or shamanism.

Strong Empathy for All Living Beings: Starseeds tend to have a deep empathy and compassion for all living beings including animals, plants, and the Earth itself. They may feel a strong urge to protect and nurture the environment and advocate for the well-being of all life forms.

Ability to Communicate with Nature: Starseeds may have a natural ability to communicate with nature spirits, devas, or elemental beings. They may feel a deep connection to the elements and have a sense of kinship with the natural world.

Experiences of Timelessness or Non-Linearity: Starseeds may experience moments of timelessness or non-linear perception, where past, present, and future seem to merge into one. They may have a sense of *deja vu* or feel like they have lived through certain experiences before.

Strong Connection to Certain Symbols or Cosmic Archetypes: Starseeds often feel drawn to specific symbols, cosmic archetypes, or sacred geometry patterns that resonate with their soul's origin or mission. These symbols may appear in dreams, visions, or synchronistic encounters.

Feelings of Isolation or Alienation: Starseeds may feel a sense of isolation or alienation from mainstream society, cultural norms, or social structures. They may struggle to fit in with conventional expectations and seek out like-minded individuals who share their cosmic perspective.

Awakening to Higher Consciousness: Starseeds may undergo a spiritual awakening or consciousness expansion process where they become more aware of their multidimensional nature and cosmic heritage. This awakening might be triggered by significant life events or inner soul prompting.

Desire for Truth and Authenticity: Starseeds often have a deep-seated desire for truth, authenticity, and transparency in all aspects of life. They may feel called to seek out deeper meanings and understandings beyond surface appearances.

Feeling of Mission Completion or Fulfillment: Starseeds may experience a sense of mission completion or fulfillment when they align with their soul's purpose and contribute to the collective evolution of consciousness. This sense of fulfillment might bring a deep sense of peace and contentment.

Resonance with Galactic or Cosmic Frequencies: Starseeds may resonate with specific galactic or cosmic frequencies such as the Schumann Resonance or cosmic rays from distant stars. These frequencies can activate dormant aspects of their DNA or consciousness.

Through exploring starseed origins and characteristics, we are reminded of the interconnectedness that binds us to the cosmos and to each other. Through the lens of starseeds, we glimpse the infinite possibilities that await us as we awaken to our true cosmic heritage and reclaim our Divine birthright.

In the presence of starseeds, we find beacons of light and wisdom guiding us toward a deeper understanding of our purpose and potential on this planet. They remind us that we are not alone in our journey but rather part of a vast cosmic family that spans the galaxies and dimensions of existence.

As we integrate the wisdom of the stars into our daily lives, we are called to embrace our own inner starseed: the spark of Divine consciousness that resides within each of us, waiting to be ignited. Through self-discovery and self-realization, we unlock the latent gifts and abilities that lie dormant until we step into our power as co-creators of our reality and stewards of the Earth.

May the wisdom of the stars continue to illuminate our path and inspire us to shine brightly, knowing that we are all starseeds traveling together toward a future of unity, harmony, and love. And may we never forget that we are, indeed, made of stardust—woven from the same cosmic fabric that binds the universe together in a tapestry of infinite possibilities.

The next chapter of this section delves into compelling hypnotic sessions conducted by Barbara Lamb and featuring individuals who have undergone regression therapy leading them to a startling realization: they are starseeds. These captivating narratives illuminate the transformative unfolding of self-discovery as they uncover their celestial origins and embrace their unique roles in the universe.

STARSEED HYPNOTIC REGRESSION SESSION #1

A young woman who interviewed me on her YouTube podcast later came to me for a regression. She wanted to know why she had always felt so different from other people she knew and why she didn't have a sense of fitting in. She said she had always been especially sensitive to energies and was able to intuitively know things about people. She felt more comfortable being alone in nature than being with others. The regression gave her significant information that helped her to understand and accept herself.

Under hypnosis, the woman went back to an experience she had at age five, lying on her bed and wondering about the universe and stars. She had always felt that her real home was out there in space. As she was doing this, she heard a voice in her head telling her she was from the stars, and that she would always be protected and guided by the beings from there. She did not know who they were, but they felt familiar and comforting. From then on, she ceased feeling so alone. Later in life, these beings from the stars contacted her in person. She previously had been aware of only the first few moments of some of those visits, but in the regression, she experienced more details of the encounters.

She has come to know, over time, that these beings are from the star systems of Pleiades and Sirius. Some of the visitors are Greys, but she feels most connected to the Pleiadeans and Sirians. She experiences them as encouraging her, protecting her, and loving her like guardian angels of a high frequency. She has always enjoyed and appreciated her experiences with them. It feels like they are always with her. She has visits from them and is sometimes taken to their ships. On one trip, they placed a small implant in her thumb. They told her it would help them to find her when they wanted to visit.

She feels a painless, electric-like sensation in that thumb when they are approaching her. She then prepares a time and place to be alone and receptive to their visit. More often, she connects with them telepathically, especially when she is meditating or walking in nature.

She has always felt these beings to be benevolent and caring about nature, the Earth, and humanity. They encourage her to fulfill her missions: educating humanity about the existence of benevolent beings and giving helpful service to her fellow humans.

She is always keeping a lookout for other starseeds so she can encourage them in completing their missions. Having left her job of several years, she is currently self-employed as a massage therapist and does healing by using a special kind of touch. She intuitively knows where her clients need extra energy, and she sends it to them. She also intuitively knows about their lives and challenges, and she sometimes advises them.

Another part of her service is providing awareness for the need of pure, high-vibrating water by using special purification equipment. She understands that this water helps people on physical, mental, and spiritual levels. She wants the best for humanity. She also educates and inspires people with her podcast and interviews with other starseed people.

She eventually discovered that she has hybrid children who live on spaceships. Her eggs and her DNA had been used to create these beings. Although it was a surprise to learn this, she said she feels honored that the beings wanted to create life by using some of her material. This further enhances her connection with the beings and her feeling of being drawn to space. She is pleased to know she has children somewhere, as she has no children here on Earth.

STARSEED HYPNOTIC REGRESSION SESSION #2

This client described herself as being dedicated to becoming closer to God and the universe and becoming the best person she can be. She gave the following details about herself.

From an early age, she sensed that she had been chosen to be here on Earth for a reason. Like many other people, she spent years trying to figure out what that reason might be. She became aware when she was young, that things are not always what they seem to be. This led to her dedication to figure out what is real and true and to determine what her role is in the universe.

She has a physical disability, and when she was a young child in nursery school she was in a class with other children who also had disabilities. She felt deep sensitivity, understanding, and empathy for the other children. She used to push the wheelchair of a little girl who couldn't walk, and she did various things to help the other children. Even at that age, she felt there was something big she was supposed to do when she grew up.

This woman has been receiving messages from higher beings for most of her life without knowing where the messages were coming from. In 2019, extraterrestrial beings appeared in her living room and said, "You need to know we are *real*. You need to act on the experience of seeing us." She realized then that they were the ones who had been giving her guidance. They had inspired her to study death, and she subsequently became a death doula.

The beings directed her to study with an Aboriginal shaman who taught her many skills and much wisdom. They have a sense of humor and show up in funny ways. They encourage her to laugh because they know she needs laughter to relieve the seriousness and stress of her work.

Two years after their first visit, she asked to see the beings again, and they complied. She had said aloud, "I want to see you!" and "Can you help me get ready to see you?"

Then she practiced for weeks to receive them and to remain calm and conscious. A month later, at an outdoor gathering of a CE5 (Close Encounters of the Fifth Kind, named after a movie with that title) group, she saw Grey alien faces in the clouds and continued to see them for three days. She also saw a seven-foot-tall humanoid figure with a big head standing in front of an evergreen hedge. She thought, *This is an energy merger*, and it went on for a while. Later, she saw more seven-foot-tall beings.

Another day, she was hiking in nature with a friend when he suddenly had to leave her alone in the wilderness for forty-five minutes while he went to get something from his car. She thought that was strange, but during his absence, she had her first sighting of a UFO, which was exciting for her. When the friend returned, he said he had felt influenced by something to leave her. She recognized that she had been receiving messages from the beings in the UFO. She continues to feel these beings when they influence her to speak out, in public talks and in writing, about the truths she has been realizing—including about their existing and visiting Earth to help humanity.

For years, she thought she was supposed to become a famous figure, like an actress, so she would be seen. As she matured, she realized she was supposed to be heard from the richness within herself. Part of her inner work now is to convey messages from her guides.

She feels a strong sense of responsibility to be of use to others. Currently, she works full time with children who are autistic or have other difficulties, even though the job is arduous and exhausting. She gets messages in her head to find and help lost or distressed animals. She is active in an animal rescue league and has done a lot of nurturing work with horses. She knows that all animals are conscious and that interacting with them is important. "It makes them happy, and it makes us happy." She believes animals are an extremely important aspect of life on Earth, and they need to have us communicate with them. She has the skill of communicating with animals telepathically. She also communicates with plants and trees. She knows all forms of life are precious.

She says she has always felt she was from somewhere else and was puzzled about the choices many people make. She knows she is here to help this planet and all life forms on it. She has always been aware that there were aspects of herself that she needed to work on.

She continues to be dedicated to working on herself, believing that everyone doing self-work would make the world a better place: "We need to start with ourselves first before improvements can be made worldwide." She would like to see everyone knowing their true power.

STARSEED HYPNOTIC REGRESSION SESSION #3

This starseed let me know that she had heard that starseeds have had previous lifetimes in places other than Earth—and she feels that she is one of them. She knew that starseeds have different capabilities because the systems they came from operate differently. They are interplanetary souls rather than Earth-based souls.

Through regressions, she learned that she has had previous lifetimes on other planets as a variety of beings, some of which had similarities to humans. Because of these past experiences of being non-human, it has been difficult for her to fit in with human life on Earth. Some starseeds are less advanced in their comprehension, but they are working their way up to a higher level of understanding. She made the analogy of the former one-room schools in rural communities where all ages of children were taught in the same room and the younger children had the advantage of learning from and with the older children.

"That is how it is on Earth among people," she said. "Starseeds are akin to the older children, helping the younger ones to learn what they would not usually know, by showing them a higher perspective."

Because of her intelligence and her ability to just know what to do in challenging situations, she became a manager in a large corporation at age nineteen. She always promoted harmony among the employees and felt she was there for their support. She rose up the ladder within the company, reaching a remarkably high position by age thirty. But then unusual things began to happen in her personal life.

She went through a dark night of the soul when a serious relationship ended and she felt overwhelming grief. In her meditations, she had visions of two previous lives with that same person, which helped her to understand the deep connection between the two of them. She also had visions of the future, including a severe car accident that would happen soon. Two days later, that accident happened, but she escaped without any harm. After that incident and a few others, she found that her knowledge about future events helped her to prepare effectively for them so the outcome would be better.

She became interested in knowing more about consciousness, and the universe revealed more to her through books and other resources. The books of Dr. John Mack stimulated a change in her view of reality, as his patients' and his view had changed because of their experiences with beings from other parts of the universe and from other dimensions. This triggered her memories of her own experiences with extraterrestrial beings, which she had been unaware of before then.

She found it overwhelming to remember these things and experienced cognitive dissonance. When she discovered Daryl Anka and his channeling of Bashar, it helped her to realize that contacts from extraterrestrial beings were real and could be benevolent and safe. This helped her to trust that her experiences with these beings were safe to explore, which she did in hypnotic regressions.

Further regressions revealed that most of her soul group—her star family—is still out there in space. They channeled a message to her: *We have always been watching and supporting you.* They continued to guide her through telepathic messages.

Our regression inspired her to go to India and learn from great masters about the practices that Jesus learned when he was there. Her guides prompted her to go to Peru to learn co-creation, manifestation, and working with the Tarot, and then to get Shamanic training. She became a Shamanic practitioner. She realized that she is on a path to transcendence and that all the spiritual practices she has been learning are helping her to be of service to people.

Since she left her company management job, she has been concentrating on offering her services to people. She works with individual people in helping their spiritual development and transformation, their personal ascension, and their evolution. She helps them see their potential. She speaks from beyond 3D reality, out of Earth time and space, with a different experience of reality.

She recognizes that starseeds come into this reality on Earth with karma from past lives, as we all do, and they are working their way up to a higher consciousness. They are helping other people to do the same. With so many people focusing on disaster prophecies and current atrocities, it is important to realize that those disasters are happening to only part of the population—not all of it. Future difficult events also might occur for part of the population.

Her advice is to send blessings to the people involved and to ask for God's support. Her overall message is this: We need to continue with our own lives and service.

STARSEED HYPNOTIC REGRESSION SESSION #4

An adult student of astrophysics told me she had memories going back to the time when she was an infant in her crib. She remembers that she and her twin sister slept in the same room, but in separate cribs. One night, two unusual beings entered their room. They went to the twin's crib and opened the sides, the way one would open a book. Then they went to my client's crib and opened it the same way and held her in their arms. Although frightened at first, she soon realized these visitors felt like family and were safe.

Her sister, now an adult, remembers these beings as tall, bluish-purple humans who were glowing. My client remembers them as glowing dragons that stood upright and had wings. Both twins experienced these beings as benevolent and loving. My client knew, even at that young age, that she would be an orator when she grew up and would bring people together in groups.

At age seven, she gave a speech to her class and felt confident and safe. This reinforced her sense that she would be doing much more speaking to groups of people. As she grew older, she did various jobs and eventually ran a successful company, where she earned a lot of money. During those years, she was completely involved in the physical world and did not pay any attention to anything spiritual.

Her perspective changed completely when she had a near-death experience (NDE) in 2015. She met and recognized her star family and the true home from which she had come. Later, she thought the beings might have caused the NDE, to remind her of who she is and what she is here in life to do. She also realized that many star beings must be living on Earth and some of them might need support. She began to recognize starseeds by their bright auras and their frequencies. She knew that their dormant DNA is from one species of beings more than from the others, and those beings activate that DNA in the starseeds, even if they don't have contact with them. Experiencers might be part extraterrestrial and/or might be having contact events with them. They are people who have made agreements with the beings at the soul level, whether they are consciously aware of it or not. This is the same with starseeds.

Currently, this woman has left her company and is back at school studying astrophysics. She feels compelled to study this field and has received messages to do so. She has been told by her guides that she would be drawn to mathematics and would be creating equations to explain the universe, to make it more accessible and understandable to people. Mathematical equations inspire thought and lead to abstract concepts. When she presents some of her original ideas about the universe to her professors, they see them as a reconceptualization of the existing understanding. She loves making the universe and extraterrestrials understandable and will be doing more of this with groups of people.

She has created a retreat center for hybrids and starseeds. Her brain is now constantly experiencing things on different levels, and it is exciting to her. Because she has dyslexia, it can be a strain to do all the reading her education requires, but her learning disability also allows her to see things from a new perspective, such as from the end to the beginning.

She can help those she works with explore their own spirituality, their extraterrestrial contacts, their off-planet heritage, their missions, and more. She knows there are many starseeds on Earth besides herself, including the starseed children. She intends to continue this outreach for people to hear from each other and discuss the subjects they cannot discuss with most of the people in their lives. She thinks there must be a frequency sent to Earth to bring people together to explore their experiences, their wonderings, and to carry out their missions. They seem to find each other and recognize each other, often with amazing synchronicities bringing them to the same place at the same time.

Her special abilities are helping her with all she does and will be doing. In her daily life now, she sees many beings and strange things. She has interactions with beings from other realms and other planets. She has strong psychic abilities, such as seeing people's problems, sicknesses, emotional states, and aura color changes. She is highly empathic and describes herself as a tuning fork because she feels other people's energies and resonates her own frequencies to other people's energetic fields. People come to talk to her about their deepest issues. She puts her hands over people and heals their auras and bodies. She talks to the other side and brings messages to people. As she expressed it, she has one foot in the next realm. Simply being near people with her special frequency seems to uplift them.

All her family members share some of her characteristics and understand what she talks about. Her mother has a noticeable glow and looks much younger than her age, as many starseeds do. She once experienced a visit from her deceased grandmother, who appeared to have large, black eyes and looked like what is known as a tall white ET. Her grandmother said, "We in our family are like this." My client found this perfectly acceptable.

STARSEED HYPNOTIC REGRESSION SESSION #5

I conducted a regression with a woman starseed who understands that she lives a multidimensional life guided by the Niburian Council of the ninth dimension. She talks frequently with her star family and receives inspiration and guidance from them. She lives by this guidance and trusts that her life unfolds in the most meaningful way possible, even when she is guided to other states and countries to meet the starseed people with whom she will be collaborating in service to humanity. When meeting them, she has an experience of immediately knowing them and knowing she can trust them.

She is aware now that when she was ages eleven through twenty, she was taken from her home and raised on a ship with her star family. She has only a few memories of those years, but it was at this time that she formed a strong bond with the Niburian beings. She gave birth to her first child, a son, when she was seventeen. She learned that she had lived many lifetimes on other planets in the Orion and Sirian star systems.

She described often feeling amazed that she is living this life on Earth, which remains strange for her. Since she returned to Earth at age twenty, she has been reconnecting with her Earth family, having relationships, and giving birth to two more children. They are in their late teenage years now and they talk frequently with her about ETs, spaceships, and other dimensions. Their friends often come to their house to see the visiting beings. The children have a reasonable understanding of why their mother is different from any of the other mothers and why she removes herself sometimes to meditate and receive messages from the Niburian beings to organize and carry out her missions.

Fortunately, her husband is also a starseed, and he accepts who she is and joins her in her mission in life. Together, they intend to buy a large tract of land and create a sanctuary where ET-hybrid children can land on Earth and be raised and taught about living life with human beings. They have enough financial resources to fund this project, and they are combining with others they are guided to meet who can help facilitate this project. They intend to create gatherings and formats for discussing important issues and raising consciousness. They also intend to help people of all ages awaken to the truth of existence and know who they truly are. They have been told that Earth is the only place where the inhabitants do not know who they are, and that we are huge, immortal souls who evolve differently in our own ways and in our own timing.

They understand that no one dies. After living here and then being in the spirit realm, we can choose which planet and which type of being we want to be. Our experiences are for the purpose of learning and evolving our souls.

This couple travels to various places in the world to activate the grid lines and to clean up generational lines. They are trying to help people choose spirituality, respect, and love of life instead of materialism, opposition, negativity, and killing life. They recognize that all people come into life as

156

babies and become programmed by the human society around them. They need to be awakened to know the spiritual beings they really are. Only starseeds come into life on Earth with a knowing that they will be changing the world.

They recognize the principle of "as above, so below" playing out in the world. There are competitions and wars going on between civilizations in space, too. Other enlightened beings are working to transform that dynamic in space.

They emphasize that the spaceships are around us all the time, blasting higher frequencies to Earth. As we raise our consciousness and our frequencies, we are able to see them and receive them more fully. It is up to us if we want to use those frequencies to create a better world.

STARSEED HYPNOTIC REGRESSION SESSION #6

From an early age, this starseed woman felt that something was watching her, but she was comfortable with it. Whatever was watching also communicated with her. Messages simply floated in during daytime or nighttime, but they were always benevolent. She understood their messages. She did not feel related to those who were sending the messages and watching her, but they felt somehow familiar to her, and she somehow knew that they came from ships in the sky. She never felt afraid of them.

She was a devoted Catholic, even riding her bicycle alone to morning Mass every day as she was growing up. Nevertheless, she welcomed the presence of these beings. She had the sense that these messages were precious and should be kept private, so she did not even talk to her family about them.

Throughout her childhood and teen years, she worked every day on her family's farm, tending to the vegetable garden. This gave her plenty of time to connect with nature and the outdoors and to be in a meditative state. Receiving messages while out in the garden seemed normal to her. She is not aware of having any visits from the beings, but she felt as if they were a part of her, and she welcomed them and trusted them.

These beings spoke to her about aspects of reality that no one else she knew spoke about. Whenever she was curious about something, they gave her answers. She did not think of them as extraterrestrial beings—which no one talked about—but she thought of them as star beings, decades before she heard anyone else use that term. She had heard of angels, but she knew these beings were something different. These helpful guides made her feel protected and guided.

She told me she just knows things from her higher self. "It's more than trusting the information…it's real knowing…which means certainty. I go where I am told to go without questioning it or needing to know why."

These beings gave her a way into the eleventh dimension, which had been closed to humanity, where she gained access to the Akashic Records. This began her decades of work with the Akashic Records. She has taught many classes and workshops on this subject and has written books about how to read the Akashic Records as well as books about the fifth dimension.

This starseed's special services to humanity include her teachings, her retreats, and the training of other starseeds. She also speaks at conferences, writes books, and teaches people how to evolve into the fifth dimension in ascension—she might have been the first person to write about this.

ECHOES OF THE STARS

A s we conclude our section on starseeds, we are left with a greater understanding of their essence, origins, and significance. Starseeds are not merely beings of flesh and blood; they are cosmic travelers, souls who have journeyed from distant star systems to incarnate on Earth with a sacred mission. They carry within them the memories, wisdom, and vibrational signatures of their celestial homelands, so they can serve as beacons of light and catalysts for evolution in a world in need of awakening.

Who are the starseeds? They are wanderers, seekers, visionaries, and individuals who feel a deep sense of longing and purpose that transcends the confines of earthly existence. They are often healers, teachers, and way-showers who are guiding humanity toward a higher state of consciousness and collective harmony. Starseeds are the embodiment of cosmic love, compassion, and unity, reminding us of our interconnectedness with all beings and the vastness of the universe within.

Where do starseeds come from? They hail from distant star systems and galaxies, each location with its own unique frequency, energy signature, and cosmic heritage. From the Pleiades to Sirius, from Arcturus to Andromeda, starseeds originate from star nations beyond our wildest imagination. They bring with them the gifts, talents, and perspectives of their celestial lineages, enriching the human experience with their cosmic wisdom and otherworldly insights.

Are you a starseed? The answer lies within your heart where the resonance of truth echoes through the corridors of your soul. If you feel a deep sense of connection to the stars, a longing for home that transcends earthly bounds, and a mission to awaken humanity to its Divine potential, you may indeed be a starseed. Trust your intuition. Honor your inner knowing. If you are a starseed, embrace the cosmic heritage that lies dormant within you, waiting to be remembered and activated.

The diverse array of hypnotic regression sessions presented here offers a fascinating glimpse into the realm of starseeds and their intricate journeys of self-discovery. Through regression therapy and deep introspection, these individuals have unearthed profound truths about their cosmic identities, illuminating the interconnectedness of humanity with the cosmos. Their experiences serve as poignant reminders of the vastness of the universe and the boundless potential that lies within each of us to explore and embrace our celestial origins.

As we reflect on the stories shared within these pages, it becomes clear that the concept of starseeds transcends mere speculation. These personal accounts offer a compelling framework through which to understand the complexities of human existence. From the moment of awakening to the realization of their cosmic heritage, these individuals have embarked on a transformative path of growth, enlightenment, and spiritual evolution.

Looking ahead, the journey of a starseed will continue to unfold, guided by a sense of purpose and a deep connection to the cosmic forces that shape our lives. As we navigate the challenges and mysteries of existence, may we draw inspiration from these remarkable narratives and embrace the inherent wisdom that resides within each of us. For in the universe, we are all interconnected threads, woven together by the timeless rhythms of creation and destined to shine brightly as beacons of light in the vast expanse of the cosmos.

In concluding our section on starseeds, let us honor and celebrate the important role they play in the grand tapestry of our existence. May we recognize the divinity within ourselves and each other and may we embrace the starseed within, shining our light brightly and igniting the flames of awakening in all beings. For in the unity of our souls lies the key to unlocking the infinite potential of the cosmos and co-creating a world of love, peace, and harmony for generations to come.

SECTION THREE
HYBRIDS

THE DAWN OF THE NEW HUMAN

In this groundbreaking exploration, we embark on a quest to unravel the secrets of hybrids: individuals who embody the synthesis of human and non-human elements, serving as vessels for the expression of cosmic consciousness and Divine wisdom. From ancient legends to modern-day encounters, we will delve into the stories, theories, and experiences that illuminate the multifaceted nature of the hybrid phenomenon.

Who are these beings and what sets them apart from the rest of humanity? Are they the products of genetic experimentation, the descendants of ancient civilizations, or the emissaries of celestial realms? As we look deeper into the heart of this mystery, we come to understand that the truth of hybrids transcends mere physicality. It is a story of souls awakening to their cosmic heritage and embracing their sacred purpose in the grand symphony of existence.

In the records of human history, a new chapter is unfolding that speaks of a profound evolution in our understanding of what it means to be human.

As we stand on the threshold of a new era, we are witnessing the emergence of a remarkable phenomenon: the rise of the hybrid.

In ages past, humanity has grappled with questions of identity, purpose, and our place in the cosmos. Yet, as we gaze upon the dawn of a new day, we find ourselves confronted with a reality that surpasses our wildest imaginations, in which the boundaries between human and non-human blur and the fabric of our existence is reshaped by the forces of evolution and transcendence.

Hybrids are the harbingers of this transformative shift. These individuals embody the synthesis of human and non-human elements transcending the limitations of conventional understanding and embracing the boundless potential of their cosmic heritage. They are the vanguard of a new paradigm heralding a future in which the barriers between the mundane and the extraordinary dissolve and humanity steps boldly into its role as steward of the cosmos.

To understand the nature of the hybrid, we must go to where ancient wisdom meets cutting-edge research, and the mysteries of the universe unfold before our eyes.

Join us as we embark on a voyage of exploration into the unknown guided by the light of curiosity and the spirit of discovery. For in the realm of hybrids, the boundaries of possibility are limitless, and the journey of self-discovery is an endless adventure into the depths of the soul.

In this chapter, we delve into the enigmatic realm of hybrids exploring their origins, their abilities, and their role in the universe as we seek to unravel the secrets of these remarkable beings and shed light on their profound significance for the future of humanity.

. . . .

Hybrids, in the context of various belief systems and speculative theories, are individuals who are believed to possess a combination of human and non-human genetic traits. The concept of hybrids often arises in discussions related to extraterrestrial contact, genetic manipulation, or interbreeding between humans and beings from other worlds or dimensions. The following are some perspectives on what hybrids might entail.

Extraterrestrial Hybridization: Some theories suggest that extraterrestrial civilizations have conducted genetic experiments involving humans, creating hybrid offspring with mixed human and alien DNA. These biological hybrids may possess advanced abilities, heightened consciousness, or unique physical characteristics inherited from their extraterrestrial ancestors.

Interdimensional Hybrids: In metaphysical and spiritual contexts, hybrids may refer to individuals who have incarnated on Earth from other dimensions or realms of existence. These hybrids may embody a blend of human and non-human soul essences, allowing them to bridge the gap between different planes of consciousness and serve as conduits for higher-dimensional energies.

Genetic Engineering: Some conspiracy theories and speculative narratives suggest that hybrids are the result of covert genetic engineering experiments conducted by government agencies or clandestine organizations. These experiments may involve the manipulation of human DNA to create individuals with enhanced physical or psychic abilities for various purposes, such as military applications or intelligence gathering.

For centuries, humanity has been captivated by the mysteries of its own origins and the possibility of connections to otherworldly realms. In the chronicles of myth and legend, tales abound of beings who embodied the fusion of human and Divine, or human and extraterrestrial, blurring the boundaries between the earthly and the celestial. Yet, in recent times, these ancient whispers have found a new resonance. Following is one such recount about the first hybrid experiment.

THE HYBRIDIZATION PROGRAMS

Throughout human history, the study of genetics has long been regarded as a cornerstone of scientific inquiry, offering insights into the complex interplay of nature and nurture that shapes our existence. Yet, as we peek deeper into the mysteries of the genome, we uncover a story that transcends the boundaries of conventional understanding—a story of hybrids and the enigmatic tapestry of their genetic heritage.

Some speculate that, at the heart of the hybrid phenomenon lies a genetic code that defies easy categorization blending elements of human and non-human ancestry in a symphony of diversity and complexity. To unravel this code is to embark on a journey of discovery that challenges our preconceived notions of what it means to be human and inviting us to explore the hidden depths of our evolutionary lineage.

In the dawn of human history, when our species was still in its infancy, our planet was visited by beings from distant stars who were drawn to Earth's burgeoning potential and the promise of new beginnings. Among these celestial visitors were many wise and ancient races who were attracted to the primordial energies of our world. They co-mingled with the earthlings and life was beautiful.

It was during this time of cosmic convergence, a harmonious merging or synchronization of various celestial elements that the Anunnaki, a technologically advanced civilization hailing from the stars, began to conduct genetic experiments on the human species. These experiments were born out of a desire to accelerate the evolutionary path of humanity and to unlock the latent potential encoded within our genetic makeup.

With their advanced understanding of genetics and biotechnology, the Anunnaki saw in humanity a canvas upon which to imprint new possibilities by blending their genetic material with that of humans. The hybrid beings they created would be easily manipulated by them.

These experiments were conducted with great care and reverence for the delicate balance of life. The Anunnaki worked to nurture and support the emerging hybrid races, fostering the pretense of a harmonious coexistence between the celestial and terrestrial realms as a guise for their later intended plans.

Yet, as with all great endeavors, the path of genetic experimentation was not without its challenges and complexities. The intermingling of humans with other extraterrestrial races brought forth unforeseen consequences and moral dilemmas.

As the experiments continued, tensions began to arise between different factions within the Anunnaki civilization, each advocating for their own vision of humanity's future. Some saw the hybrids as a way to uplift and empower humanity, while others viewed them as tools of manipulation and control.

Amidst these conflicting agendas, the fate of the now-hybridized human races hung in the balance, their destiny intertwined with the broader currents of cosmic evolution. As the experiments unfolded, some of the new creations transcended the limitations of individual species.

Witnessing what was occurring to the people of Earth, the angelic beings, Arcturians, Andromedans, and other benevolent races, visited the Anunnaki to urge them to stop their experiments. Angelic beings felt it was morally wrong to manipulate the genetics of a race and supersede their free will. But the Anunnaki had already spliced their own and other malevolent races' genetics with the humans. The solution of the benevolent races was to add their genetics to the mixture also. Now humans had both types of DNA, ensuring the sovereignty of free will.

Frustrated by their defeated efforts, the Anunnaki created the idea to manipulate the people of Earth to think that they were separate from Source, so they would believe that they were alone and should be fearful. By influencing humanity to believe false perceptions, they could allow their free will but still alter the trajectory of their decision-making processes.

To support their efforts, they set in place a piezoelectric field that, when compressed upon the crystalline grid surrounding the Earth, would imprint codes designed to lower the frequency of human thinking. Their endeavors were fortified by the energetic nexus between the crystalline grid and the intricate network of crystalline ley lines that traverse deep within the Earth. Humans didn't stand a chance as these codes cocooned them from both above and below. This field also decreased the Earth's vibrational frequency and lowered it to a third dimensional planet. All the other inhabited planets in our solar system were in the fifth dimension. This created the false matrix.

Could the Anunnaki genetic experiments have created humans as they exist today? If so, to what degree? Did the DNA of the benevolent races restore balance to the human genome? Are we all hybrids or did some of us evolve independently of these influences?

There are many theories about hybridization, genetic engineering and the creation of the human race as we know it. Whether through subtle energetic shifts or direct genetic alterations, humanity's true origins might involve a more complex interplay between cosmic forces and our Earthly evolution than we ever thought possible.

Currently, there are no Anunnaki occupying the Earth, yet the results of their hybrid program continue.

HYBRIDIZATION SIGNS

Like walk-ins and starseeds, signs indicating someone might be a hybrid can vary and often manifest in subtle or unusual ways. Here are some insights into potential signs of hybridity:

Heightened Sensitivity: Hybrids may exhibit heightened sensitivity to energy, emotions, and the environment around them. They may be more attuned to subtle shifts in energy and possess an intuitive understanding of the world.

Unusual Physical Characteristics: Some hybrids may display physical traits or features that differ from those of their immediate family or ethnic group. These traits could include unique eye colors, distinctive facial features, or anomalous body proportions.

Profound Spiritual Awakening: Hybrids often undergo a profound spiritual awakening or existential crisis leading them to question the nature of reality and their place in the universe. They may feel a strong sense of longing for connection with higher realms or extraterrestrial beings.

Unexplained Memories or Dreams: Hybrids may experience unexplained memories, dreams, or visions of otherworldly landscapes, beings, or technologies. These experiences may feel vivid and real yet defy conventional explanations. They also experience frequent visitations from the genetic material donor(s) and welcome the visitations.

Feeling of Alienation: Hybrids may struggle with feelings of alienation or not fully belonging to Earthly society. Many feel that they do not belong to their biological family and long for their *real* family. They might feel like outsiders or misfits, longing for a sense of home or belonging that eludes them.

Exceptional Abilities or Talents: Some hybrids may possess exceptional abilities or talents that surpass those of their peers. These abilities could include heightened intuition, telepathy, psychic abilities, or advanced cognitive skills.

Unexplained Healing Abilities: Hybrids may exhibit unexplained healing abilities or a natural affinity for energy healing modalities. They might feel drawn to alternative healing practices and possess a knack for facilitating healing in others.

Attraction to Cosmic or Extraterrestrial Themes: Hybrids often feel a strong attraction to cosmic or extraterrestrial themes in art, literature, film, or spirituality. They may resonate deeply with stories of contactees, abductees, or star beings, feeling a personal connection to these narratives.

Sensitivity to Energies: Hybrids may experience heightened sensitivity to energies including electromagnetic fields, geomagnetic anomalies, or fluctuations in Earth's energetic grid. They might feel physically or emotionally affected by these energies, experiencing symptoms such as fatigue, dizziness, or mood swings.

Purposeful Mission or Calling: Hybrids may feel a sense of purpose or calling to contribute to the evolution of humanity and the planet. They might feel driven to advocate for social or environmental causes, promote spiritual awakening, or facilitate healing and transformation on a global scale.

Feelings of Observation: Some hybrids describe a sense of being caringly observed—not in an unsettling way, but as if they are being gently and attentively watched.

It is essential to approach these signs with an open mind and discernment, recognizing that everyone's journey is unique. While these signs may suggest hybridity, they do not definitively confirm it. The exploration of one's identity and experiences is a deeply personal and ongoing process.

HYBRID PHYSICAL FEATURES

To elaborate more on the physical features of hybrids, signs can vary widely, depending on their genetic human and extraterrestrial heritage and the specific characteristics engineered into their biology. Here are some potential physical traits that hybrids may exhibit:

Shape of Eyes: Many hybrids will have eyes shaped much larger than a regular human eye.

Unusual Eye Color: Hybrids may have unique eye colors not commonly found in their family lineage or ethnic group. These could include striking shades of blue (10 percent), true green (2 percent), violet (less than 1 percent) or gold (5 percent), or even heterochromia (1 percent), where each eye is a different color.

Distinctive Facial Features: Some hybrids may possess facial features that differ from those of their immediate family members or ethnic background. These features could include high cheekbones, elongated faces, or pronounced jawlines.

Blood Type: Many hybrids will have unusual or rare blood types.

Height and Build: Hybrids may display variations in height and body proportions compared to their family members. They may be taller or shorter than average with slender or more muscular builds that deviate from familial norms. There may also be unusual bone and muscle consistency.

Uncommon Hair Texture or Color: Hybrids might have hair textures or colors that stand out, such as unusually thick or fine hair, or shades of vivid red, silver, or platinum blonde not commonly seen in their family trees.

Skin Tone: Skin tone can vary among hybrids with some individuals having fairer or darker complexions than their relatives. They may exhibit a unique glow or luminosity to their skin, giving them a radiant appearance, or their skin may have shades of green, blue, or gold tints.

Subtle Markings or Symbols: In some cases, hybrids may bear subtle markings on their bodies such as birthmarks, freckles arranged in geometric patterns, or faint scars that seem to hold deeper significance.

Exceptional Symmetry or Proportions: Hybrids may possess exceptional symmetry or proportions in their facial features and body structure, giving them an aesthetically pleasing appearance that stands out from the norm.

Unusual Physical Resilience: Some hybrids may demonstrate remarkable physical resilience or adaptability to their environment with enhanced immune systems, quicker healing times, or increased tolerance to extreme temperatures.

Longevity: While not always apparent in appearance, some hybrids may exhibit signs of extended longevity or slower aging compared to their peers, suggesting genetic modifications that promote longevity.

Ethnic Ambiguity: Hybrids may exhibit an ambiguous or mixed ethnic appearance, making it difficult to pinpoint their ancestry based on physical appearance alone. This ambiguity could stem from the blending of genetic material from multiple human and extraterrestrial sources.

It's important to note that these physical features are not exclusive to hybrids and may also occur naturally in the human population, due to genetic variation. Additionally, the presence or absence of these traits does not definitively confirm or rule out hybridity, as individual experiences and genetic makeup can vary significantly.

HYBRID MOTHERS

Many women today continue to report involvement in the hybridization program, where they claim their pregnancies were augmented or that they have been taken aboard extraterrestrial craft for genetic experimentation. These testimonies describe how their eggs are harvested and used in various reproductive procedures. Typically, the process unfolds in one of three ways.

In one method, the woman's eggs are extracted and combined with the sperm of both a human male and an extraterrestrial male to create a hybrid embryo. This embryo is then placed in the human woman's uterus and the woman becomes pregnant. After approximately two months of gestation, the developing fetus is removed and taken to the craft. It is placed in a special liquid-filled tank, where it gestates to full term and is born by being removed from the tank. Once the baby is born the human mother is occasionally brought back to the craft to meet her hybrid baby for the purpose of the infant receiving the mother's nurturing and love. The beings have learned that since the baby is partly human that they need some human affection to survive.

In another process, the woman's egg is fertilized directly by an extraterrestrial male through sexual intercourse. The fetus is either extracted and progresses similar to the above or it is allowed to mature inside the mother, allowing the pregnancy to progress naturally. The child, born as a hybrid with both human and extraterrestrial traits, is raised on Earth. However, many of these children are often taken aboard a craft to interact with their extraterrestrial parent(s) and to engage with other hybrid children.

The third reported method involves a human pregnancy that is later altered by extraterrestrial intervention. After a few months of gestation, the woman is taken aboard a craft, where the fetus is injected with extraterrestrial genetic material via a needle inserted through her abdomen and into the uterus. Following the procedure, the woman may either return to Earth to give birth or remain on the craft until delivery. I know of a woman who states as a fetus she was injected with genetic material from seven different races while her mother was aboard a craft.

Some hybrid mothers even claim that, despite having had their wombs removed, they were implanted with an embryo in an artificial womb placed inside their bodies. These women then carried the fetus to full term, either aboard the craft or back on Earth.

Many of these mothers note that their hybrid children possess distinctive physical or energetic characteristics, seemingly designed to accommodate higher vibrational frequencies associated with extraterrestrial souls.

Determining if you are a hybrid mother can be a deeply personal and complex experience, often requiring introspection, self-awareness, and exploration of one's experiences and feelings. Here are some steps you can take to explore this possibility and seek support if you believe you may be a hybrid mother:

Reflect on Your Experiences: Take time to ponder any unusual or unexplained experiences you may have had throughout your life such as vivid dreams, encounters with unidentified beings, or feelings of connection to otherworldly realms. Pay attention to any intuitive insights or gut feelings that suggest a deeper connection to the cosmos.

Seek Out Information: Educate yourself about the phenomenon of hybridization and the experiences of hybrid mothers. Research online forums, books, and documentaries that discuss the topic and connect with others who may share similar experiences.

Keep a Journal: Start documenting your unusual or significant experiences, dreams, synchronicities, or intuitive insights. Recording your thoughts and feelings can help you gain clarity and identify patterns or recurring themes that may point to hybrid motherhood.

Consult with Experts: Consider seeking guidance from professionals who specialize in topics related to hybridization, extraterrestrial contact, or spiritual awakening. Psychologists, therapists, hypnotherapists, or regression therapists experienced in working with individuals who have had anomalous experiences may offer valuable support and validation.

Connect with Support Groups: Join online or local support groups for individuals who identify as hybrid mothers or have had extraterrestrial contact. These communities can provide a safe and understanding space to share your experiences, receive validation, and connect with others who may be on a similar journey.

Work with Energy Healers: Energy healers, shamans, regression therapists, and holistic practitioners who are open to metaphysical concepts may help in exploring your spiritual connection and integrating any extraterrestrial or cosmic energies you might be experiencing.

Trust Your Intuition: Ultimately, trust your intuition and inner guidance as you navigate this adventure of self-discovery. Allow yourself to be open to new insights and possibilities. Honor your unique path and experiences without judgment.

If you feel overwhelmed or distressed by your experiences, it's essential to seek support from compassionate professionals who can provide guidance and assistance tailored to your needs. Remember that you are not alone.

There are resources and communities available to support you in your self-discovery and integration as a hybrid mother.

In this chapter, we delved into the genetic landscape of hybrids seeking to understand the origins and implications of their unique genetic makeup. In pondering these beings, we continue to uncover the threads that weave together the intricate tapestry of their existence, shedding light on the mechanisms that govern their physical and metaphysical attributes.

Central to our exploration is the concept of genetic hybridization—the process by which genetic material from two or more distinct species or populations intermix to produce offspring with novel traits and characteristics. While traditional notions of hybridization often evoke images of crossbreeding between different animal or plant species, the phenomenon of hybridization introduces a new dimension to the equation, blending human and non-human genetic material in ways that challenge our understanding of evolutionary biology.

We do not know exactly what constitutes a hybrid being or how to determine their genetic identity. At its core, the genetic makeup of a hybrid is characterized by a blending of human and non-human DNA resulting in a hybrid genome that reflects the diverse influences of their cosmic lineage. This genetic diversity may manifest in a variety of ways from physical traits and abilities to spiritual gifts and intuitive insights that transcend the limitations of ordinary perception and cannot be detected with traditional scientific means.

Yet, despite the inherent complexity of their genetic makeup, hybrids do not seem to be simply products of chance or genetic experimentation. They are beings of purpose and intention born of a cosmic blueprint that transcends the confines of ordinary understanding. Their genetic heritage reflects their soul's journey through the cosmos, encoding within it the wisdom, experience, and potential of countless lifetimes spent traversing the galaxies and dimensions of existence.

As we journey deeper into the genetic landscape of hybrids, we are reminded of the intricate interplay of nature and nurture that shapes our collective destiny. The genetic code of a hybrid is a testament to the boundless potential of human evolution, offering glimpses into a future where the boundaries between human and non-human dissolve, and the full spectrum of our cosmic heritage is embraced with reverence and awe.

As we conclude our exploration of the hybrid phenomenon, we find ourselves at the threshold of profound and captivating hypnotic regression sessions. The intricate interplay between human and extraterrestrial energies woven into the fabric of our existence beckons us to delve deeper into the mysteries that lie beneath the surface.

Who knows? Science may yet uncover the hidden truths of our cosmic lineage and the profound significance of hybrids in the unfolding story of human evolution.

In the following section, Barbara Lamb describes her own discovery process in learning about hybridization through hypnotic regressions of her clients. Then, Lamb will continue with her case studies of individual clients and their experiences.

AWAKENING THE HYBRID SECRET

Hypnotic regression has long been a powerful tool for uncovering hidden memories and deeper truths about one's identity. When it comes to those who identify as hybrids, these sessions often reveal profound insights and transformative experiences that can lead to a deep understanding of the soul. Through the lens of the following regression sessions, we get a glimpse into the complex and multifaceted nature of hybrid beings. These sessions not only uncover repressed memories but also provide a pathway for hybrids to reconnect with their origins and understand their unique role in the broader cosmic tapestry.

Beginning in 1991, when conducting hypnotic regressions with people who were having encounters with extraterrestrial beings, I became aware that many of them had hybrid children who were part human and part extraterrestrial. Extraterrestrial beings had removed eggs from the women and sperm from the men. The eggs and sperm had been combined with extraterrestrial genetics to form an embryo, and the embryo was then implanted in the woman's uterus. In some cases, the hybrid fetuses had more extraterrestrial genetic material. These were removed after two months of gestation and placed in a gestation tank on a spaceship. Some were removed when they were ready to be born, raised and educated on the ship. They spent their lives assisting the beings who had created them.

After several years, I learned of hybrids who were living here on Earth. They had been created in the same way but were left in the women's wombs for the full term of the pregnancy. These hybrid babies were born on Earth in the usual human way. They grew up and continued their lives as fully human, although they contained extraterrestrial genetics as well as human genetics.

During subsequent years, I learned many aspects of the hybridization programs were carried out by a variety of beings. I learned how they created hybrid babies. Some of the babies were growing up and being educated on spaceships and some were growing up here. I learned the purposes for creating the hybrids who lived on the ships: Some were destined to save the dying races of extraterrestrial beings by adding our more robust physicality. Some were intended to make up for their inability to reproduce offspring, caused by too many centuries of cloning and by collecting too much radiation during space travel. Some hybrids were created to correct genetic mistakes made during hybridization with other species.

Other purposes for hybridization included: enabling the hybrids to stay on Earth longer; for gaining the component of emotion and creativity that humans have; becoming suitable to settle on Earth if their planets became unlivable; and developing the capability to go between living on Earth and living on other planets while understanding both as ambassadors. Some hybrids were created to perpetuate the human race, in case our species becomes extinct from destroying our Earth. Others were intended to upgrade the human race by introducing higher intelligence, greater psychic skills, and a sense of group cooperation.

Some of my clients reacted favorably when they became aware of having hybrid babies who lived on spaceships. They had a strong motherly or fatherly feeling for these beings and were happy to see them every year or so as the babies were growing up. Some of the mothers wished they could bring their babies home to Earth and raise them here, but they were told those babies were not human enough to survive here. Some were delighted to discover they had many hybrid babies—in one case, a woman had thirty-five offspring! Some men and women wanted to form a private community in a remote area where they could raise hybrid children who could be brought to live on Earth.

However, other parents were shocked and disturbed by the appearance of the babies and wanted nothing to do with them.

For several years, I assumed all hybrid babies lived on spaceships or other planets. Then, to my great surprise, at a large UFO conference, I met a woman who reminded me of a hybrid. When I said that to her, she confirmed "I am a hybrid!" I came to know her well and admired her tremendously. She was making sculptures of several different types of extraterrestrials while channeling from the beings exactly what they looked like. These statues were reported by those who bought them to have the special abilities of communicating with them and inspiring them. This woman helped many star beings to recognize who they were and what their special work was. I was thrilled that such a wonderful hybrid being was living here on Earth.

Two years later, I met another hybrid woman and immediately recognized her as a Mantis being. She affirmed "Yes, I *am* a Mantis being. I came from Planet Estigan!" She stayed with me for a week and I became thoroughly convinced that she was a hybrid with many special abilities. She was co-leading weekend workshops and support groups for star being children and their parents. She said she felt led to identify and inspire star children as she went about her life.

Very soon thereafter, I was contacted by a woman who recognized she was a Reptilian hybrid. She was proud and happy to be one, and she said her husband had some reptilian DNA and accepted hers. She belonged to a reptilian church that met in an underground facility. She said she shapeshifted into her full reptilian form when she experienced intense emotion. She sent me some photos of her performing in an opera. At the intense emotional moments of the opera, her face appeared to change its texture to reptilian texture and patterning and her eyes appeared to have vertical slits for pupils.

I was invited in 2011 to present a lecture to the national Mutual UFO Network's annual symposium on the subject of ET Hybrids: Are They Real? Are They Here? This meeting focused my attention even more on the hybrids living among us. Three of my hybrid regression clients had appeared in their pure reptilian forms; I gained validation of this from witnesses. For these hybrids, shapeshifting was a magnificent experience that they hoped to repeat.

During hypnotic regression, one of these women recalled being taken to an underground military facility and studied/observed in her full reptilian form by three military men through a two-way mirror. She was proud of being her reptilian self but disliked the circumstances of being studied without her agreement.

I was subsequently invited to attend two weekend gatherings of other hybrid people and was pleased to get to know several of them. I was impressed with the quality of these people, feeling they were brave to be here as hybrids. I admired their unique abilities and the service they were giving to humanity. These were normal-looking people and were delightful to know.

Right after this, I began receiving phone calls from a writer in England, Miguel Mendonca, asking me to tell him everything I knew about hybrids. He knew a few hybrids in England and was especially interested in them. We decided to write a book together, which we eventually published and titled

Meet the Hybrids: The Lives and Missions of ET Ambassadors on Earth. We did long interviews together with eight hybrids and I conducted regressions with them.

Most of these people had been hybridized by their mother's eggs and father's sperm being taken and mixed with the beings' DNA. These embryos were implanted in the mother's wombs and carried full term and were born here on Earth in the way that the rest of us were born. In a few cases, hybridization was accomplished when the pregnant mothers were five or six months into gestation and were injected with the beings' genetics through the wall of the abdomens and uteruses and into the fetuses. They looked like normal human babies and continued to look human. Thereafter, they grew up in their human families and went to school like the rest of us without anyone knowing about their extraterrestrial genetics. From very early ages they each felt that they were not from here and their families were not their real families. They felt their true families were somehow out in space. They missed these beings and longed to see them. They were happy when their beings did visit and took them on board their crafts. Through their regressions and those of their parents, they learned how they had been created. Some also got this information through extraterrestrial beings telling them.

From their earliest awareness, these hybrid children feel different than everyone else around them. They are disturbed by the density here. They intuitively know things that other people do not. They see auras around people's bodies and can feel the physical infirmities experienced by people. They know what people are thinking and feeling. Some can move things with their minds or heal people and animals by sending energy through their hands. They have many psychic abilities, including clairvoyance, clairaudience, and clairsentience. They always want to help people, and they find many ways of doing so. They sometimes get messages from their star families.

Some of these hybrids have unusual physical characteristics, such as non-typical blood types, unusual bone consistency, weaker muscles, different skin texture, and organs being in unusual places in their bodies. One woman I know has thumbs that are wider at the end, which helped her to make her sculptures.

They each have missions that they are trying to accomplish such as doing psychic work; physically healing people and teaching them how to be healers; giving intuitive readings; fostering spiritual awareness and growth; and inspiring people to do the work they came into life to do. They feel they are here to raise the consciousness of humanity and to prepare people for the forthcoming process of ascension. They are also here to create positive awareness of extraterrestrial and other-dimensional life forms. Their purpose is to raise the consciousness of humanity so that humans can be accepted into the intergalactic community: the great Galactic Federation.

The hybrids do this work by teaching classes, giving presentations, consulting with individuals, hosting conferences, writing articles and books, holding support groups, creating podcasts, presenting information on websites, and doing physical healing. They each emphasized that we are all one and are part of the Great Creative Source. I believe we are truly blessed to have these hybrids among us.

On the following pages, I will share with you a few of the hybrid regressions that I have conducted.

HYBRID HYPNOTIC REGRESSION SESSION #1

A woman who had been part of a secret space program of the United States government came to me for a regression, wanting to know more about herself and what her purpose was in life. She knew she had been to other planets in that program and had made contact with extraterrestrial beings. She also remembered having contact with these beings while on Earth.

She knew she was part of a group which plans to take large groups of humans to settle on other planets. They will take only people who intend to perpetrate good and will live peacefully and cooperatively with the beings who already live on those planets. According to her understanding, they will be quarantined for two weeks when they arrive there. If they have any medical problems, they will be healed on special medical beds. She felt honored to be chosen for this program and was excited to leave her life on Earth and to live in a whole new way. She felt this would be an ascension of consciousness and not a removal from her physical body.

During the regression, she learned many details about this program that she had signed up for. She learned that space beings are not allowed to interfere with a civilization unless there is a threat of extinction of that civilization. They see Earth as having that threat. Because they had created the human species long ago and had watched over them for millennia, they did not want humans to end. Therefore, they were taking certain humans who would continue living on other planets when the Earth would no longer sustain mankind. The people they were choosing to take were each hybridized with extraterrestrial genetics so they could survive on the other planets and successfully relate to the beings there.

She also learned during the regression about how and when she had been hybridized. She had been born fully human and had been taken during early infancy to a secret laboratory where humans were working with beings from space. They injected extraterrestrial DNA into her as a newborn to determine if she would be able to survive space travel and life on another planet as part human and part extraterrestrial. These beings, who also worked with the secret space program, informed her parents about my client being a hybrid and having some of the ETs' genetics. This inspired them to bring her into the program during her childhood and continuing through her adult years.

Her father, who was in the U.S. military, had been involved in this secret military/civilian program. He essentially donated his child for this clandestine project. He and the other humans in this project also wanted to study my client to see if she would be able to relate to and cooperate with the ET beings and to learn more about the ET mentality. My client's mother knew about this hybridization of her baby. She accepted it because the baby was especially alert, intelligent, and responsive. After the regression, the mother corroborated this to my client.

My client had contact with ETs throughout her life, some of which she had consciously remembered before coming for the regression. The beings were mostly Pleiadians and Arcturians.

During the regression, she learned more details about those contacts and about other encounters of which she had been unaware. She recalled her first UFO sighting at age ten when on a camping trip and relived the details of the beings walking around on the ground and taking her onboard their spacecraft.

At age twenty, she was taken to an underground lab near Dulce, New Mexico where humans and two reptilian beings injected her with a blue/green liquid to enhance her ET genetics and make her more adaptable for space travel.

Even though her hybridization was primarily intended to help her travel through space and live on a different planet, she discovered she had many talents that she might not have had and which she is effectively using here on Earth. She is especially intuitive and has an impressive array of psychic skills. She is proficient in healing people and animals. She attempts to educate people about the existence of space beings and aspects of reality that most people are not aware of.

She does this through broadcasts about these matters and interviews with other people who know about them. She has a following of people who have had these unusual experiences and want her support. She is trying to inform as many people as she can and to raise the consciousness of humanity.

She currently describes herself as one-quarter human, one-quarter Blue Arcturian, one-quarter Pleiadian, and one-quarter Alpha Draconis.

HYBRID HYPNOTIC REGRESSION SESSION #2

A regression with one woman answered many questions that she had been wondering about for years. Under hypnosis, she relived an event that had happened during her adult life. She had been sleeping in her bed one night when she woke up and sensed someone in the room. She saw a little girl with what looked like sunglasses on and gradually realized the sunglasses were big, black eyes. This child was small and frail and had blond hair. A slightly bigger girl was there too, and she had the same kind of eyes. A younger boy with similar eyes seemed to be floating in the air near them. These children remained for a while and gradually came closer to her.

They telepathically communicated with her. She knew they were not human, yet they appeared sort of human. They seemed happy to be with her, and she was happy to see them, although their visit came as a surprise.

The children were familiar to her because, for many years, she had taken trips to their spaceship. She remembered watching them being taught lessons by a tall Mantis being, in a classroom full of children of various ages and appearances. She realized they must be hybrid children and a mixture of various non-human races. They all seemed healthy and well cared for as they paid total attention to their teacher. She had the sense that they were doing well in life, and this pleased her.

She wanted to see the three child visitors more often because she sensed they were her children. She remembered a few times when she had gone to their spaceship, which was just outside our density. She had chosen to go there in her astral body, as she was familiar with astral travel to many different places, including out in space. Sometimes, she had been guided to the spaceship by extraterrestrial beings. Both the children and adult beings on their spaceship seemed to enjoy her visits. The hybrid children had to lower their frequencies to come here to Earth and it was difficult for them to hold our frequencies. It was decided that it would be better for her to raise her frequencies to match theirs and to visit them on their ship.

In this regression, she also learned about how she became a hybrid. Her mother had considered her a miracle baby because she had been unsuccessful for many years in becoming pregnant. Tests revealed that she produced no eggs—so her eventual pregnancy came as a complete surprise. After my client was born, according to her mother, Jesus came to her and assured her my client would be okay, even though she was born prematurely. He said she was here for a special mission: to help humanity get on the right track and raise their frequencies.

Eighteen months later, the miracle happened again, and her mother gave birth to a baby boy. The mother had been visited many times by extraterrestrial beings. They had removed her eggs and stored them for years until the correct time for her to bring these babies into the world. In each case, they had mixed an egg with the father's sperm and their DNA and then implanted it as an embryo in the mother's uterus.

My client and her brother were natural musicians and both grew up to make music their careers. Her brother composes songs, she sings and writes lyrics, and they perform this music together. They have developed a large following and have performed in many countries with the mission of raising consciousness. They understand that this is what the beings want humanity to experience, but the beings cannot survive here to accomplish this. My client and her brother feel they are ambassadors by doing this work.

HYBRID HYPNOTIC REGRESSION SESSION #3

A woman from Italy did a regression with me online. She had always felt so different from everyone else, and she wondered, "What is the point of being alive?" The regression took her back to her childhood. It revealed that she had been receiving messages and visits from her cosmic family beginning at a young age. In one of the visits, seven beings stood in front of her and activated her chakras. Even though she did not understand chakras, the activation felt pleasant and she understood that they seemed to care about her. These were tall, androgynous beings with white skin. They were silent as they were sending energy to her chakras, and they seemed to be performing some sort of ceremony. To her the process seemed special and sacred.

The beings said they were there to check on her and to be sure she was okay. They told her they were her cosmic family, and this felt true to her. She had never felt her Earth family was her real family and she had longed to be with her true family. She felt that she had been one of these extraterrestrial beings but was subsequently born on Earth as a human. They confirmed this and were loving and caring. She received telepathic messages from them during that visit and thereafter, even when they were not visible to her.

In the regression, she also relived her birth experience in a clinic here on Earth. There was not enough fluid in her mother's body to help her move through the birth canal, so the delivery took a long time. While her mother was in labor, the obstetrician took a break to eat his Easter lunch. She intuitively knew he was annoyed with her for taking such a long time to leave her mother's body. Her twin brother was in the womb with her, but he died before being born. This caused further complications and delays. His soul decided to stay with her and entered her infant body, where he remained for life. She realized in the regression that this made her a "two-in-one" being.

Before this regression, she had never liked her body. It somehow felt not right, even though she looked like other girls. She felt she had not received enough education for being a human, even though she didn't know what that meant. In the regression, she realized her cosmic family had injected their DNA into her when she was in her mother's womb. Her soul had come from another dimension, and she had been a different kind of being. She had not been prepared enough to live a human life in a denser dimension and in a physical body. She thought her hands looked strange, because as a cosmic being, she had had only three fingers on each hand. On Earth, she had a different kind of body than her cosmic family had, which she had vaguely remembered and compared herself unfavorably to.

When she had been in her crib, sometimes her cosmic family came in the form of a cloud and picked her up. She enjoyed this feeling and accepted that it was happening. This contrasted with being picked up by her human family, which she did not like at all. She did not like being touched by humans, even though they wanted to touch and hold her. She often felt confusion about the visits from her cosmic family. Were they happening when she was dreaming or while she was awake? In any event, she welcomed them and felt their love.

She had always looked for her real mother, as she intuitively knew her human mother was not it. She used to ask if she had been adopted and she was always told, "No." Her Earth parents had some physical problems. She assumed that if she developed those problems, it would mean she must be their daughter. Eventually, she did develop a couple of those problems, so she assumed she was biologically part of that family, although she did not feel like it.

When she is in the cloud with her real family, she told me, she feels like a giant insect with huge, green eyes, completely white skin, blond hair, a tiny nose and mouth, and no ears. She relived an experience during childhood of going to a classroom on a ship and the other kids who were her friends looked like her insectoid self.

She said, "We breathe light, not air. We do not eat. We don't talk with our mouths and voices. We communicate telepathically. My friend on my left looks like an insect with a tiny body and long arms and legs. She has a body like a wasp. Her face is angular, and her eyes are large. The friend on my right side is a Mantis, an insect type of being, and taller than me. She has large, round eyes, all black and no pupils. A friendly Mantis being is teaching us. He is very tall, and his arms are extra-long and fold over from his wrists."

She remembered that back on Earth, she did not talk until she was age three or four. There was no need to speak because she knew what everyone was thinking. People thought she was mute or something was wrong with her. Eventually, she realized she should speak like everyone else, and she learned how.

In the regression, she was told by one of the teacher beings that she needed to write a book about her unusual experiences and her being a mixture of beings (a hybrid). She was to inform other humans about the existence of other kinds of intelligent beings and about other dimensions of reality. They realized that most humans do not know about those aspects and are limited in their understanding of reality. Her writing and broadcasting would expand humanity's awareness of other beings and prepare them for the beings who would eventually show themselves more publicly on Earth. This is her mission: to inform people and prepare them for accepting other kinds of beings and working cooperatively with them for good purposes.

HYBRID HYPNOTIC REGRESSION SESSION #4

A woman in England approached me online for a regression because she was trying to understand the unusual things she had been experiencing since her childhood. She had awakened many nights to see a bright light coming through the window of her bedroom followed by an awareness of an exceptionally tall man with blue eyes, long blond hair, a handsome face, and slightly pointed ears. She assumed he was human, but because he did unusual things—such as suddenly appearing and disappearing—she wondered what else he could be. She discovered that she could understand what he was saying, although she heard his words in her mind, and he could understand what she was thinking. Even though these visits were confusing to her, she welcomed them and felt cared for. Nobody believed her when she talked about that man. People thought her story was strange, so she remained silent about the man and his visits throughout her childhood and teenage years.

At a conference, she met a woman who was a hybrid, and many aspects of this woman matched what my client had been experiencing. She began to wonder about herself. Her kinesiology teacher had tested her for her psychic and healing abilities and determined that these abilities were unusually strong. The teacher also recognized that my client had strong spiritual awareness and interest. At the teacher's instructions, she began to draw mandala designs which she had been seeing in her mind's eye and found them to be spiritually enlightening. After drawing the mandalas, my client had more visitors in her room at night.

Our regression answered many of her questions. One night, she was taken through a tube of light up through the ceiling, through the air, and into a spaceship. Then she was taken into a room and was transformed temporarily into one of the beings who had escorted her. She wore the same kind of clothes: a long, royal blue robe with a stand-up collar. They told her she was one of them, and was part Pleiadian, part Sirian, and part human.

The beings said they had created her by injecting her with their genetic material when she was in her mother's womb. They had done this so they would have an emissary on Earth who would be motivated to do the work that needed to be done but which they were not be able to do themselves. Even though they looked mostly human, they would not be able to survive on Earth more than a few minutes at a time. They assured her they would give her guidance in carrying out her mission if she would develop a regular practice of meditating.

She accepted the assignment and recognized that she had unknowingly been preparing for it by studying neuropsychology and understanding the human mind. She was already working as a clinical psychologist and neuroscientist.

In a star origin reading, my client learned that she had been Pleiadian in previous incarnations. She had had a great ability to heal other beings, and she had brought those abilities into this lifetime. One night, when her Pleiadian visitors were in her room, she felt intense heat coming from her hands. The visitors told her the heat was healing energy and she could use it to heal other people. They also pointed out various psychic abilities she had and encouraged her to use them to help her fellow humans.

After the regression, she began to notice that during her meditations and while doing mindless tasks like washing dishes and doing laundry, she was also receiving messages from her Pleiadian guides. They were always encouraging and full of helpful guidance. She was impressed at how well they understood the human psyche. She took their messages seriously and applied them to her work with people. After a while, she felt a constant connection with the beings.

As she got used to being a hybrid, she recognized she had always felt different from other people and had hated being a human. It had always deeply bothered her that there was so much meanness in the world and so many things that people did to harm and even destroy and kill others on such a huge scale. She had noticed that other people were bothered by those aspects, too, but they were better able to put them out of their minds and go on with their lives.

During her regression, she realized that people do destructive things because of the way their minds work, and one of her tasks is to reconstruct their way of thinking. She also recognized that she must have had powerful guides rescue her, because she had been in three catastrophic car accidents without having been physically harmed.

She currently likes being a hybrid and is grateful for the help her fellow beings give her. She is relieved to feel assured that she is doing the work in the world that she came into life to do. She wishes to form a worldwide community of hybrids to understand and support each other and to stimulate ideas for being even more helpful to humanity.

HYBRID HYPNOTIC REGRESSION SESSION #5

When a thirty-five-year-old man came for a regression, he already knew he had been having visits from extraterrestrials since early childhood. He felt he had a close relationship with some of them, especially with the Mantis beings. He had unusual wrists that folded over parallel with his inner forearms. People in his martial arts class pointed out that he used his hands in a unique way. His friends joked with him about this feature and nicknamed him "Mantis."

He said he frequently saw praying mantis insects staring right at him in his garden and on windowsills and doorknobs, looking as if they wanted to communicate with him. They reminded him of the tall Mantis beings who often visited him at night. He had always felt the beings were benevolent, even when they took him away from home and onto a spacecraft. He often noticed odd markings on his body, and he felt small, round objects under his skin and one under his tongue, which he eventually learned were implants.

He learned, during his first two regressions with me, that he was a hybrid being with a large percentage of DNA from Mantis beings although he also had Reptilian, Tall White, and Sirian DNA. He realized that those were the beings who had visited him through the years. He noticed that they had a collective consciousness and yet were able to communicate telepathically with his singular consciousness. He mostly identified with the Mantis beings, who were kind and well-meaning. He described them as having soft-textured bodies with fat rolls and enormous, black eyes that wrapped around the sides of their heads.

These beings told him they had created him as a hybrid by taking eggs from his mother and sperm from his father and then adding DNA from a few different species who were working together. They implanted the embryo they created in his mother's womb. There was another embryo in the womb, having been conceived in the normal, human way. His mother was told she was carrying twins, but the other twin disappeared from the womb by the time my client was born. It was a mystery to his mother and to the medical personnel.

My client had always felt something was missing in his life and someone else was supposed to be with him, without knowing about the missing twin. Learning about this helped him to understand those feelings he had been having. He wondered if the twin was the one who sometimes moved things around and left hints that someone was there. The beings assured him that the twin was living with them on the spaceship with other children who were hybrids.

The Mantis being said his species had existed forever and had created many other species. They had been successful in combining Mantis genetics with other types of beings. The intention was to create more and more types of intelligent, benevolent lifeforms to improve the lives of residents on various planets. My client wondered if his own ancestors had received genetic modifications, making him a hybrid by heritage as well. Knowing about his being a hybrid answered many questions he had always had about differences he noticed between himself and other people.

This man is aware of receiving guidance from the Mantis beings. Ten of them seem to be around him most of the time. They guide him with gentle thoughts, but they know he needs to figure out things for himself. They urge him to think loving thoughts and to train himself to do this by remembering times when he had felt especially loved and loving in the past, feeling it in his heart and sending it out to others. This is important for balancing the negativity and bad feelings and actions going on in the world. They emphasized that he and others can do this, and it will make a difference. They said that, with his higher frequency, he is raising the love frequency of others around him, just by his being here.

The beings have also told him they had made an agreement with his soul just before he came into this lifetime to be a hybrid and work with their guidance to help humanity raise its consciousness. They pointed out various aspects of his mission in his life: (1) Being an ambassador between their species and humans, and bringing awareness of the beings to more people, preparing them to meet and trust these beings. (2) Becoming accustomed to being a human since he had previously been other kinds of beings in previous lifetimes. (3) Helping the extraterrestrial beings to understand what it is like to be a human, since they can see through his eyes and know his thoughts. (4) Helping experiencers to understand their experiences with the beings and how to deal with them. (5) Teaching people to initiate contact with the beings if they want to do so. (6) Teaching people to protect themselves through using visualization if they feel such a need. (7) Doing holographic healings, and teaching others to heal and meditate. (8) Making sacred geometric jewelry for activating people. (9) Inventing and making energy devices. (10) Organizing gatherings for hybrid people and starseeds where they can share, discuss, and plan how to collectively help humanity.

CROSSROADS OF CREATION

In this section, we explored hybrids through a collection of personal tales about extraordinary experiences. By learning about hybrids through information shared during hypnosis, we have traveled through realms of the unknown that sheds light on the understanding of humanity.

The story of how the first humans may have been created serves as a pivotal point of departure, inviting us to contemplate the notion that humanity may be more intricately connected to the cosmos than we ever imagined. The idea that our genetic code might bear traces of extraterrestrial influence challenges us to reconsider our place in the grand narrative of the universe. It beckons us to explore the possibility that our existence is part of a cosmic tapestry, intricately woven together by beings from realms beyond our comprehension.

Learning about hybrid mothers adds a deeply human dimension to the narrative. The stories of these women, who claim to have given birth to hybrid offspring, bring forth questions of identity and show us profound love transcends terrestrial boundaries. Their experiences compel us to consider the depths of the maternal instinct and the idea that motherhood extends beyond the confines of Earth, spanning the cosmos itself.

The exploration of hybridized bodies challenges our understanding of genetics, evolution, and the potential for coexistence with extraterrestrial civilizations. It raises questions about the boundaries of the human form and the adaptability of our species. These stories can be seen as a testament to the resilience of life and its ability to evolve in response to the ever-changing dynamics of the cosmos.

Hypnosis can be a tool to unlock memories of hybrid experiences. Hearing the information uncovered during hypnosis invites us to consider the possibility that our consciousness is not limited to the surface of awareness but extends deep into the recesses of our psyche, where memories and experiences may lie dormant, waiting to be unearthed.

In conclusion, the exploration of hybrids and their origins, hybrid mothers, hybridized bodies, and the power of hypnosis propels us into the abyss of mystery. It challenges us to expand our horizons, to question the boundaries of our understanding, and to embrace the mysteries that surround us.

As we navigate the uncharted depths of these narratives, we must remain open to the possibilities that lie beyond our current knowledge. The enigma of hybrids reminds us that the cosmos and the depths of human potential are still waiting to be explored.

EMBRACING THE COSMIC TAPESTRY

These stories of walk-ins, starseeds, and hybrids have traversed the vast landscapes of human consciousness uncovering the threads that weave these enigmatic phenomena into the tapestry of our existence. The previous chapters delved into the intricacies of each topic, shedding light on the mysteries that blur the boundaries between the ordinary and the extraordinary. But this is only the beginning.

The concept of walk-ins introduces the profound implications of soul exchange for a higher purpose. It challenges us to contemplate the nature of identity and the fluidity of the soul's journey. Through the accounts of those who have undergone these transformative experiences, we learned of the intense shifts that can occur when a soul crosses the threshold into a new existence.

Starseeds, as souls from distant celestial realms, beckon us to look beyond the confines of our terrestrial abode and to entertain the idea of complex civilizations elsewhere in the universe. These stories remind us to consider the vastness of the universe and the interconnectedness of all beings as we contemplate our role in the cosmic dance of existence.

Hybrids, residing at the crossroads of humanity and the unknown, invite us to question the essence of our species. As we delve into the possibilities that genetic splicing and the presence of off-Earth species might be part of human history, we have to ask if we are now facing a new chapter in human evolution. Could hybrids be on the forefront of the physical changes happening in the human species right now?

Yet, for all that we have shared, we are keenly aware that there is still much left to explore. The realms of walk-ins, starseeds, and hybrids stretch out before us like an endless horizon, inviting us to venture further into the unknown.

During a profound conversation with my collective, we delved into the timeless mysteries surrounding the inception of all existence. They shared with me a fascinating perspective: that at the genesis of everything, there exists a deep yearning within Source to immerse itself in the experience of creation. This notion of "the beginning" became more than just a distant concept; it was an intimate desire for self-discovery.

Their descriptions painted a vivid picture of the universe as the embodiment of Source, akin to the intricate strands of DNA encoding life itself. It was a revelation that sparked a profound shift in my perception of reality.

In their wisdom, my collective revealed that Earth DNA is a pinnacle of cosmic diversity, boasting a remarkable collection of landscapes, flora, and fauna—a microcosm of the universe's boundless wonders. It is the best the universe has to offer. They conveyed that each of us carries the ancient codes of Source woven intricately into our being, akin to the universal DNA that courses through every atom of creation.

Moreover, they spoke of genetic experiments that have shaped our collective journey on this planet, hinting at a deeper connection between humanity and the celestial realms. This notion led to the realization that, in some ways, we are all hybrids and to some extent, we are all starseeds, because we carry within us the cosmic heritage of countless galaxies.

Yet, despite the profound truths we uncover, acceptance and validation remain elusive. The revelation of our galactic origins awaits the unveiling of evidence by a visiting member of our cosmic family, a disclosure that may be withheld by earthly authorities. This raises poignant questions about the nature of truth and acceptance. What would it truly mean for humanity to acknowledge its place within the vast cosmos?

Until such a pivotal moment arrives, we continue to experience the mysteries of existence guided by the whispers of the stars and the timeless wisdom of our collective consciousness. In our quest for understanding, we can navigate the realms of possibility while still embracing the enigmatic beauty of our cosmic heritage.

But let us not be overwhelmed by the vastness of our journey, for it is in the pursuit of knowledge that we find our greatest fulfillment. With each step we take, we come closer to unraveling the mysteries that lie at the heart of our existence and with each revelation, we are reminded of the boundless potential that resides within each one of us.

In the words of the ancient sages, let us venture forth with open hearts and open minds, for it is through our exploration of the unknown that we truly come to understand the vastness of our own potential. In doing so, we not only illuminate the mysteries of the universe but also the mysteries of our own souls.

May you find inspiration in the diverse narratives and perspectives presented, and may these revelations spark a flame within guiding you toward a deeper understanding of your own role in the grand tapestry of existence.

For in the exploration of walk-ins, starseeds, and hybrids, we embark on a quest not only into the depths of the cosmos but also into the boundless expanses of our own potential as beings of light and wonder.

GLOSSARY OF TERMS

Ancestral Patterns: Ancestral patterns are recurring themes, behaviors, or tendencies that are passed down through generations within a family lineage. These patterns are believed to originate from shared experiences, traumas, beliefs, and cultural conditioning that influence the behavior and mindset of family members across time.

Behavioral Patterns: Behavioral patterns refer to recurring sequences of actions, reactions, or responses that individuals exhibit in various situations or contexts. These patterns are formed through a combination of biological factors, environmental influences, past experiences and learned behaviors. They often operate at a subconscious level shaping how individuals perceive, interpret, and interact with the world around them.

Cellular Imprinting: Cellular imprinting is the process by which cells within the body retain memory or information from past experiences, events, or environmental influences. This concept suggests that cells can store and transmit information beyond their genetic code that impacts their structure, function, and behavior. Through various mechanisms, such as epigenetic modifications and biochemical signaling, cellular imprinting can influence gene expression, protein synthesis, and cellular responses.

The phenomenon of cellular imprinting plays a significant role in shaping an individual's physical health, emotional well-being, and overall vitality. Negative effects can be addressed through holistic healing modalities aimed at releasing stored trauma and restoring balance to the body's energy systems.

Cellular Memory: Cellular memory refers to the theory that cells within the body possess the ability to retain memories of past experiences or traumas independent of the brain's cognitive processes. According to this concept, cells store information about physical and emotional events that can influence physiological responses and behaviors.

While the exact mechanism of cellular memory remains a topic of debate, proponents suggest that it may contribute to phenomena such as muscle memory, organ transplant recipients experiencing memories or traits of their donors, and the persistence of certain health conditions linked to past traumas. Exploring cellular memory offers insights into the intricate connections between mind, body, and consciousness, shedding light on the holistic nature of human experience and potential avenues for healing and self-discovery.

Crystalline Grid: The crystalline grid is a network of energetic lines or pathways that surrounds and permeates the Earth. The grid, which is composed of crystalline energy, acts as a matrix of higher vibrational frequencies, facilitating spiritual evolution, consciousness expansion, and the transmission of healing energies across the planet.

Collective Consciousness: The collective consciousness is like a big web that connects all people's thoughts and feelings. It's made up of what we all know, believe, and feel, which shapes how we see the world and where we fit into it. This web reflects our shared past and our hopes and dreams, making us better understand and care for each other. Each person adds unique ideas to this big picture, making it richer and helping to decide where we're all going.

Current Timeline: A dynamic and interconnected series of events, experiences and developments unfolding in the present moment. The current timeline is shaped by the collective actions, decisions, and influences of individuals, societies, and the natural world. It's like a flowing river, constantly changing course as new currents of circumstances, ideas, and technologies converge and diverge, shaping the landscape of our shared reality.

Extraterrestrial Being: Any being from anywhere other than 3D Earth.

False Matrix: A piezoelectric field that compresses the crystalline grid of the Earth, created to instill in the collective consciousness the notion that humans are disconnected from the Prime Source, inducing a sense of isolation and fear. Creators of the piezoelectric field meticulously devised strategies to influence humanity's perception to subtly steer the course of their decision-making processes, while preserving the concept of free will.

A piezoelectric field refers to the electric field that arises in certain materials when they are mechanically deformed or subjected to mechanical stress.

Holographic Toroidal Matrix: The holographic toroidal matrix is a conceptual framework that describes the interconnected and multidimensional nature of reality. It suggests that the universe is structured like a torus, a donut-shaped geometric form wherein energy flows in a continuous loop, creating a dynamic and ever-evolving field of information.

This model proposes that every point within the toroidal field contains information about the whole, reflecting the holographic principle. It posits that reality is holographic in nature, meaning that each part contains the entirety of the whole and that the toroidal structure serves as a blueprint for the organization of energy and consciousness at all levels, from subatomic particles to galaxies. This holistic perspective emphasizes the interconnectedness of all things and suggests that consciousness plays a fundamental role in shaping and co-creating our experiential reality within the holographic toroidal matrix.

Incension Process: The process of the soul entering the body and firmly anchoring into the physical form.

Karmic Patterns: Karmic patterns are recurring themes or cycles in our lives that stem from unresolved experiences, emotions, or actions from past lives or ancestral lineage. These patterns are believed to be governed by the principle of karma, which suggests that our present circumstances are influenced by the consequences of our past actions.

Ley Lines: These energy lines are invisible alignments that crisscross the Earth's surface, connecting sacred sites, landmarks, and natural features. These lines are believed to carry spiritual or mystical significance and may serve as conduits for subtle energies, influencing the energy of the surrounding environment.

Master Oversoul: A master oversoul is a higher-dimensional collective consciousness that oversees and guides the evolution of individual souls and soul groups that make up a soul family. The master oversoul facilitates the growth and expansion of members of the group, helping them to fulfill their unique potential and contribute to the greater unfolding of universal consciousness.

Meridians: Meridians are pathways in the body through which vital energy, known as *qi* or *chi*, flows. In traditional Chinese medicine, these pathways are believed to connect various organs and systems influencing overall health and well-being. Acupuncture and acupressure techniques aim to balance and unblock the flow of energy along these meridians to promote healing and wellness.

Miasmic: Miasmic patterns refer to deeply ingrained and often unconscious energetic imprints that arise from unresolved emotions, traumas, or negative experiences. These patterns are believed to accumulate over time and can become embedded in a person's energetic field influencing their thoughts, emotions, behaviors, and life circumstances. Miasmic patterns are thought to be stored within the energy of the DNA.

Monad: A monad refers to a fundamental unit or indivisible entity that represents the essence or core of an individual's being. It is often associated with the concept of a Divine spark or soul and represents the highest aspect of consciousness and spiritual evolution. Some people, depending upon their beliefs, interchange the words oversoul or soul with the monad.

Morphogenic Field: The morphogenic field is a concept proposed in the field of biology and metaphysics popularized by biologist Rupert Sheldrake. It refers to an invisible, dynamic field that surrounds and interconnects all living organisms, influencing their development, behavior, and evolution. This field is believed to contain the collective memory and information of a species, shaping its patterns of growth and behavior across time and space. It is a kind of blueprint or template that guides the formation and organization of living systems from the molecular level to the level of entire ecosystems.

Parallel Realities: Parallel realities, also known as alternate realities or alternate universes, suggest the existence of multiple, coexisting realities or dimensions beyond our own. These realities may differ from our own in various ways, including different outcomes of historical events, alternate versions of individual lives, or entirely distinct physical laws and properties.

Past Lives: Past lives refer to the belief that an individual's soul has lived multiple lifetimes in different physical bodies throughout history. This concept is central to various spiritual and religious traditions including Hinduism, Buddhism, many Native American theologies, and certain New Age beliefs.

Planes of Existence: The planes of existence refer to different levels or dimensions of reality beyond our physical world, each characterized by unique energies, consciousness, and inhabitants. These planes are believed to coexist alongside our reality and may include the physical, astral, mental, and spiritual dimensions, among others.

Soul (Lower Soul): The soul is the most dense form of the higher self. It attaches to the body and becomes the personality of this lifetime.

Soul Fragment: A portion of a soul that individuates from its source.

Soul Integration: Soul integration refers to the process by which a new soul—or new aspects of a soul—merges with or raises the frequency of its new body and life. Soul integration may involve adjustments in personality, interests, and life direction as the walk-in's presence becomes more pronounced and integrated over time.

Soul Resonance: Soul resonance is the harmonic alignment or vibrational attunement between individual souls or between a soul and universal energies. It is the frequency at which the soul vibrates.

Source Energy Consciousness: The consciousness of Source that permeates everything—every universe, galaxy, planet, and everything on every planet.

Source-Conscious Monad: A Source-conscious monad is the ultimate essence or core of individual consciousness, directly connected to the universal Source-energy consciousness or Divine consciousness. It represents the highest level of awareness and unity with cosmic intelligence. This monad is the eternal spark of Divine consciousness within each being that guides its evolution toward self-realization and unity with the source of all existence.

Source Conceptual Plan: This term refers to the fundamental blueprint or design that originates from the highest universal or Divine intelligence—often simply called Source. This plan is thought to underlie all of creation and governs the evolution and development of the universe at both the macrocosmic and microcosmic levels.

Spiritual Bodies: The spiritual bodies of a human refer to non-physical aspects of the self that extend beyond the material realm. These bodies are often associated with different layers of consciousness and energy including the etheric, astral, mental, and spiritual bodies. Exploring and nurturing these spiritual dimensions is integral to spiritual growth, self-awareness, and a deeper understanding of one's existence beyond the physical form.

Subconscious: Referring to the part of the mental processes that operate below the level of conscious awareness.

Superconscious: The deepest level of the mind, where the highest levels of awareness and connection to something outside of us is located.

Here is a brief example: Think of the mind as a layered cake. The top layer is the conscious mind, where your awareness is located. This layer allows you to think and make decisions. The middle layer is the subconscious mind, where the emotions and memories are located. The bottom layer is the superconscious mind, the foundation structure supporting both the conscious and subconscious levels.

MEET THE AUTHORS

SHEILA SEPPI

Sheila Seppi is a soul-exchange walk-in who entered the body of a thirty-eight-year-old mother with three children, and experienced instantaneous healing from documented illnesses. She emerged with new spiritual gifts and memories, transforming her life completely.

Her first soul experience was in the angelic realm with the Elohim, where she was given the name Nawaila (Na-wai-la) by her original star family. Sheila's soul is a blend of Angelic, Pleiadian, Arcturian, Sirian-Lyran, Mantis, and Andromedan lineages, among others. She initially entered the body as and in alignment with her Arcturian frequency but has since fully integrated her Andromedan self. Sheila's mission, guided by her collective known as the Yahni (Yah-knee), is to be a way-shower, helping humanity to spiritually awaken and evolve.

In 2019, Sheila published *Walk-Ins: Cosmology of the Soul*. She is an international speaker, event coordinator, multidimensional life coach, holographic alchemist, light language linguist, regression therapist, shamanic practitioner, and spiritual teacher. Sheila uses higher dimensional frequencies to empower others to embrace their higher selves.

Sheila founded the Conscious Awakening Network and SpiritWay Wellness. Her goal is to help people spiritually remember who they truly are.

www.sheilaseppi.com
www.consciousawakeningnetwork.org

BARBARA LAMB

Barbara Lamb is a licensed psychotherapist (recently retired) and a current hypnotherapist and regression therapist. She is considered one of the world's leading authorities in the field of UFOlogy and extraterrestrial contact. Since 1991, she has also regressed countless numbers of people to some of their past lives.

Barbara has been a featured lecturer at dozens of conferences throughout the US and abroad. She has given hundreds of interviews for television programs, including Ancient Aliens and Netflix, and radio interviews on Coast-to-Coast AM Radio, GAIA TV, films, YouTube, the Conscious Awakening Network, and the internet. She has received five Lifetime Achievement Awards from five major conferences for her work in giving help and support to experiencers of ET contact and furthering the field of UFOlogy.

She is an author and has co-authored *Crop Circles Revealed, Alien Experiences, Meet the Hybrids, Kids' Adventures with ET Friends in Space* and now, *Cosmic Convergence: Journeys of Walk-Ins, Starseeds, and Hybrids.*

Barbara is an avid researcher of the crop circle phenomenon and has personally visited more than 1,800 crop circles in England since 1991. She has given many lectures and interviews about this subject and has conducted crop circle tours.

www.barbaralambregression.com

Made in the USA
Las Vegas, NV
05 December 2024

13437265R10142